AMERICAN SIGN LANGUAGE FOR BEGINNERS

AMERICAN SIGN LANGUAGE FOR BEGINNERS

LEARN SIGNING ESSENTIALS IN 30 DAYS

Rochelle Barlow

PHOTOGRAPHY BY James Bueti

ROCKRIDGE
PRESS

For general information on our other products and services or to obtain technical support, please contact our Customer Care Department within the United States at (866) 744-2665, or outside the United States at (510) 253-0500.

Rockridge Press publishes its books in a variety of electronic and print formats. Some content that appears in print may not be available in electronic books, and vice versa.

Interior and Cover Designer: Emma Hall
Art Producer: Meg Baggot
Editor: Erin Nelson
Production Editor: Jenna Dutton
ASL Model: Jocelynn Only

Photography © 2020 James Bueti.
Styling by Bethany Eskandani.

ISBN: Print   978-1-64611-642-3
         eBook 978-1-64611-643-0

R0

Mama & Daddio—thank you for giving me
every opportunity to live my dreams.

CONTENTS

BEFORE YOU BEGIN

My ASL adventure has had a lot of twists and turns, but it all began with a book. My interest began when my Grandmama read *Koko's Kitten* to me, a book about a gorilla who learns sign language, opening her to a world of empathy—and a very sweet relationship with a series of cats. I also read books about Helen Keller and devoured every ASL dictionary I could find.

My mother recognized my deep love of sign language and the ASL community and did everything she could to support my growth. I learned on my own, had a private tutor, and later took classes in high school and college. I began interpreting at the age of 17 and tutored my college classmates in a variety of ASL classes and functions. After college, I volunteered in the Deaf community and spent my days immersed in the language.

I've interpreted for more than 15 years total, mainly in the higher education system. When I had my own children, I started teaching individuals and families in their homes and in community centers. Seven years ago, I moved my teaching to my website so that I'd be able to help more people learn ASL accurately, efficiently, and respectfully.

As I said in the beginning, books are powerful and beautiful, and they have transformed my life. I hope that this book will be a similar transformational tool for you. Learning a language doesn't always feel easy. There were times when I wanted to give up, when I was frustrated, overwhelmed, and unsure of what to do next.

My mission in the ASL world is to make learning sign language as easy, inclusive, and fun as possible for you. If you've found yourself unsure of where to start or struggling to find an easy-to-follow resource, you've come to the right place. Here you'll find 30 days of lessons with straightforward instructions, original images, and useful memory tips. Lessons progress in difficulty and build on one another, and each will teach you the signs and phrases you need to engage with the world.

I believe in the power of practice, so each day you'll find an activity to help that day's lesson *stick*. The activities—all under 20 minutes—also give you a chance to combine and build upon the previous lessons for greater understanding. As you enter the rich world of ASL, take it one day at a time, one lesson at a time. After 30 days, you'll be well on your way to understanding and communicating using ASL with those with whom you want to engage most.

ASL Facts and Origins

ASL is a visual language based on specific hand gestures, with placement relative to the body along with head and body movements, mouth morphemes (the specific movements your mouth makes to add meaning to a sign), facial expressions, and other non-manual markers. We express ASL with our hands, body, and face and receive it with our eyes. Sign language grammar is structured quite differently from English grammar. It is a robust, expressive, and evolving language, with as much information expressed as any oral language.

American Sign Language is used only in the United States and Canada, so it is not a universal sign language. As you cross North America, you'll find regional signs, or dialects, just as you would hear various accents and slang across the same regions.

While American Sign Language's history is long, its journey to existence was rocky. The Deaf were considered non-persons for many centuries before variations of sign language made communication more available to the public. Charles-Michel de l'Épée, known as the Father of the Deaf, created an educational method for others to learn sign language in the 1700s. In 1815, Laurent Clerc, a French Deaf teacher educated in l'Épée's methods, met an American by the name of Thomas Hopkins Gallaudet who was also searching for a way to educate the Deaf. In 1816, Gallaudet invited Clerc to come to the United States, where he taught Clerc English and Clerc taught Gallaudet sign language. They established the first school for the Deaf in Hartford, Connecticut, where it still stands today.

Americans have used ASL ever since, but language experts did not recognize it as a true language until 1960. We still have a long way to go to support the Deaf community in social, political, and economic representation in the United States and around the world.

ASL DIALECTS

You'll hear a variety of accents as you cross the United States, indicating the speaker's home region or state. ASL has a similar phenomenon, except with signs.

ASL dialects, or regional signs, exist all over the United States. People from New York may use different signs than people from communities in Mississippi or California. ASL is used in Canada as well, so Canadians have their own dialect. Another popular dialect is Black American Sign Language (BASL).

Awareness of these dialects and regional signs is important in order to respect each person's unique ASL experience. This book does its best to represent the most common form of each sign. When you sign with these in your local Deaf community, you may see some signs done differently, but do not panic! Learning the common variation and the local dialect will make your signing flexible and varied. You should feel confident using the sign that those in your local community use most.

SIGNING GENDER

There are signs that are directly related to specific genders, such as MOM, DAD, GIRL, and BOY. These signs are located on specific areas of the face. Female signs are located on the bottom half of the face near the chin, and male signs are located at the top half near the forehead. Neutral gender is around the ear. For instance, to sign COUSIN when there is no gender referenced, you place the sign beside the ear rather than the chin or forehead.

Society is growing more inclusive of all people, no matter their gender or any other identity, so you will want to be aware of these signs and be respectful to all people. These are fairly new terms, and as these and other terms we use to identify with evolve, new signs will be added to the ASL vocabulary. The best way to discover new and relevant signs is to be involved in the Deaf community. The Deaf community is inclusive, direct, and kind, so you do not have to fear asking others within it how to sign anything.

If you are ever in doubt about how to sign something in terms of gender or other sensitive topics, fingerspell the word you want to use rather than trying to sign it to decrease the possibility of hurting another person's feelings.

THEY: With your dominant hand in the 1 handshape, start with the hand pointing across your body to the non-dominant side. Sweep your hand in front of your body. You can sign this generally, or if you are referring to a specific group of people, begin the sign in front of the first person and end the sweep at the last person.

Who Is This Book For?

This book is for anyone with a desire to learn ASL. If you have a family member or friend with whom you want to communicate, you are a civil servant, or you engage with Deaf and Hard of Hearing people in your community, this book is written for you.

You may run into members of your community who have varying degrees of hearing loss at the store, the bank, the hospital, or in an emergency. Even minimal ASL knowledge will open doors for greater communication and support of the Deaf community's human rights. Starting with basic ASL knowledge will make you a more supportive family member and a better friend or representative of people with hearing loss.

ASL is a robust, evolving, and living language. Although this book is a supplement and a resource for anyone wanting to learn American Sign Language, it is not a replacement for deeper learning. Get started here, and once you've finished, check the Resources section (page 170) for recommendations to further your ASL learning.

How to Use This Book

In part I, you'll learn foundational signs and phrases. You'll start with the alphabet—the most important place to begin signing—and then move to lessons that will serve you as you move into the world. Lessons become more complex as you go, drawing upon knowledge from previous lessons. You'll learn signs in the order of importance and utility. After Day 22, you'll enter part II, where we will focus on ASL grammar—a vital part of sign language. You'll take a deeper look in this section at the sentences you learned in part I.

The goal of this book is to provide you with signing basics and help you support the American Sign Language community. While it will best serve you to go in order, you can also feel free to bounce around by subject; just scan the Contents (page vii) to hop around or look to the Index (page 171) as a dictionary reference. Lessons include beginner phrases and related vocabulary, so you'll be able to use new words in context no matter what lesson day you are on.

You'll find memory tips, learn related or mistaken meanings for signs, and practice activities to reinforce what you've learned. Throughout the lessons, you may see a lowercase "fs" attached to a word in all capital letters. When you see this, it means the capitalized word is to be fingerspelled.

As you learn the signs, watch yourself in the mirror to make sure you're reproducing them correctly. If you're new to ASL, you'll form a new relationship to your hands, face, and body, and you might find you're not as in control as you thought! Some students think their hands are in one position, and when they look in the mirror, they realize they're not. Take the time to verify your signs in the mirror or make a video of yourself signing.

Once you can recognize and sign each lesson here, you will have mastered your first 30 days of essential ASL instruction. Repeat the lessons as many times as you need, and come back and review the material to keep it fresh. Spread out your review of the material over a short period of time, and then return later to check your retention.

As you progress through the lessons, make a note of the signs you've mastered quickly as well as those that give you trouble. Celebrate your successes and review the troublesome signs until they too are part of your ASL arsenal.

THE FIVE PARAMETERS

Each sign you'll learn has five parameters that you'll need to pay close attention to as you go through the book. The five parameters are handshape, palm orientation, location, movement, and non-manual markers. A slight difference in any one of these parameters will change the meaning of the sign.

HANDSHAPES

Each sign is composed of one, two, or more handshapes. This is the shape that your hand is in to form a sign. If you change the handshape of a sign, you can alter the meaning significantly. For instance, in WHITE and LIKE, every parameter is the same except for the handshape. There are many ASL handshapes. Here are the most common handshapes you'll see:

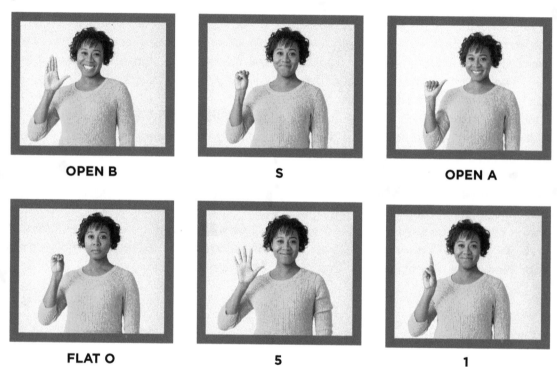

OPEN B **S** **OPEN A**

FLAT O **5** **1**

PALM ORIENTATION

Palm orientation means the direction your palm is facing. Your palm can be up, down, to the side, toward your body, or at a specific angle. Sometimes a sign can start with one palm orientation and move into another. Be aware of these changes.

STAR

SOCK

LOCATION

Every sign has a specific location. A sign can be in one location or more than one. It can start in one place and end in another. For instance, you sign MOM in one location, but when you sign WOMAN, it begins in one spot and moves to a second location. This is one of the most common differences between signs.

MOM

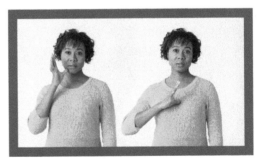

WOMAN

MOVEMENT

There are multiple types of movements your signs can make. They can be stationary, tap, twist, circle, wiggle, shake, or a combination of any of these movements. Movement is a big part of what makes signing so much fun. It really makes the visual elements pop and the picture clear.

COLD

NON-MANUAL MARKERS

"Non-manual markers" means all additional elements that add meaning to the sign that are not done by the hands or arms. The sign wouldn't mean the same thing without these elements. For instance, you sign NOT YET and LATE with the exact same four parameters, except you additionally stick your tongue out to the side for NOT YET. It's such a simple change with a big impact.

NOT YET

LATE

Non-manual markers can involve your mouth, your eyebrows, or your face.

Facial expressions are a vital part of sign language. Think of them as the inflection in your voice and the punctuation in your writing. Without inflection in our voices, it would be difficult to determine the true meaning of what someone says to us. Are they angry, sarcastic, tired, scared, or asking a question? It's the same with punctuation. Without it, we wouldn't know when to pause, consider, respond, or understand when a thought ended.

Non-manual markers, and facial expressions and body language in particular, are sign language's inflection and punctuation. You will learn how to use these and add them into your signing throughout the workbook. While it is important, it is easy to master and fun.

Facial expressions are to ASL as punctuation is to the written word. That is to say, necessary and important. You can use them to show sarcasm, boredom, elation, terror, and every other emotion with your face. If you don't reveal emotion with your facial expressions, the person you're signing with will not pick up on your full meaning. For example, you could sign you're so happy about your doctor's appointment, but without the appropriate facial expressions, your friend won't know you're being facetious.

Throughout the lessons you'll be prompted when to use your facial expressions and given more information on how to use them correctly. Use them. Play around with them. Practice in front of a mirror. If you practice your facial expressions and signs simultaneously, they'll become natural and easy to use.

You cannot express your true meaning without the necessary facial expressions and, in many cases, other non-manual markers. Non-manual markers are other types of expressions that aren't done with your hands. These are facial expressions, mouth morphemes (shapes your mouth makes with certain signs), and body language.

FINGERSPELLING

Fingerspelling—using ASL letters to spell out English words—is an important aspect of ASL. Sign language has a large vocabulary, but there are still many English words that do not have a direct sign or that use abbreviations. Proper nouns are fingerspelled. Sometimes people will fingerspell a word for emphasis.

The fingerspelling rules:

Don't bounce your hand up and down or knock it forward.

Don't say each letter as you fingerspell it; rather, say the entire word you're spelling.

Accuracy is more important than speed.

Keep your hand facing forward unless you're signing the letters G and H.

Aim for smoothness between letters.

The good thing about fingerspelling is you can practice it anywhere and anytime. In this book, you'll get practice fingerspelling starting with the very first lesson. For later lessons, you'll use your alphabet knowledge to fingerspell things like locations and names. You'll see this in the lessons as "fs" then the word, for example, "fs LOCATION."

Part I

BASIC SIGNS AND PHRASES

Day 1: The Alphabet

Welcome to your first day of ASL practice! Thoroughly grasping the ASL alphabet—knowing each letter on sight—is the foundation of strong signing. The more you know your letters, the better your sign production will be. The letters form many of the handshapes that you will see in these first 30 days of signing.

I recommend spending at least 20 minutes here each day, but give yourself permission to spend as much time as you need to master each letter. This applies even if the ASL alphabet is not new to you; the goal is to get these foundational letters down pat.

Make sure your hand is facing the exact way and your fingers are shaped the same as you see in the image. It's important to work on knowing each letter receptively (with your eyes) and expressively (with your hands). Spend an equal amount of time practicing each letter each way. If you sign facing the mirror, you can check for accuracy while also practicing the alphabet receptively.

Activity

Drill your alphabet until you can fingerspell it in 30 to 45 seconds. Practice it forward and backward. Practice common letter combinations, such as "th," "-ly," "-ed," "-ing," "-sh," "ea," and so on. First fingerspell short words and your name. Once you are comfortable with these words, practice fingerspelling common words you use every day, including places, titles, locations, streets, cities, and names.

Day 2: Number Basics

Time: 10 minutes

ASL numbers are all done on your dominant hand. Numbers 1 to 5, when signed in isolation, are signed with the palm facing you. Some numbers, such as 6, may feel strange to you since the signs don't look like what you're accustomed to when counting off on your fingers. For instance, the common W shape that people often use to show the number 3 is actually a 6 in ASL.

Numbers 10 to 29 have special signs, which is why they are pictured here. The higher numbers in the 10s and 20s can seem strange and confusing when you first learn them because the signs represent a completely new way of thinking of numbers. Remember that this is a foreign language. You wouldn't expect yourself to learn your numbers in Mandarin perfectly in just a few minutes, and you shouldn't expect to master your ASL numbers in a short amount of time either.

Once you get to 30, just sign the first digit and the second digit; you don't need to worry about a special sign. If you sign a string of numbers, such as a phone number, you do so with the palm facing out. To sign double numbers, such as 22, 33, and 44, you will face your palm down, tap the fingers down, and then arch to your side and tap again. You'll see this in the image for the number 22. Treat any double numbers from 22 on up in the same way.

Activity

Grab a handful of small items—buttons, beans, coins, cereal, etc.—and count them using your ASL numbers. Increase the number of objects you count as you get more comfortable with 1 to 10, then 1 to 20, and higher. You can also count by 2s, 3s, and 5s each time you run through this activity.

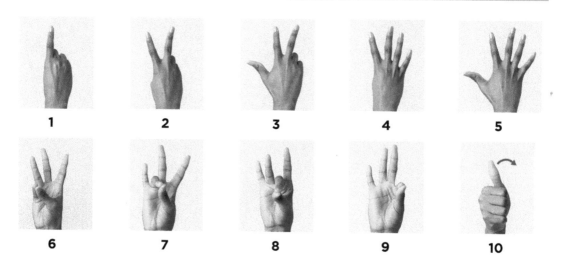

| 1 | 2 | 3 | 4 | 5 |
| 6 | 7 | 8 | 9 | 10 |

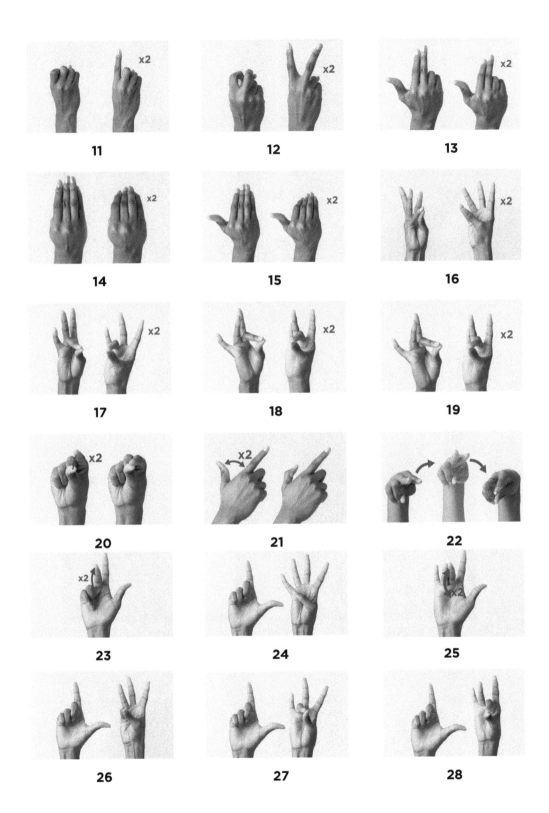

11

12

13

14

15

16

17

18

19

20

21

22

23

24

25

26

27

28

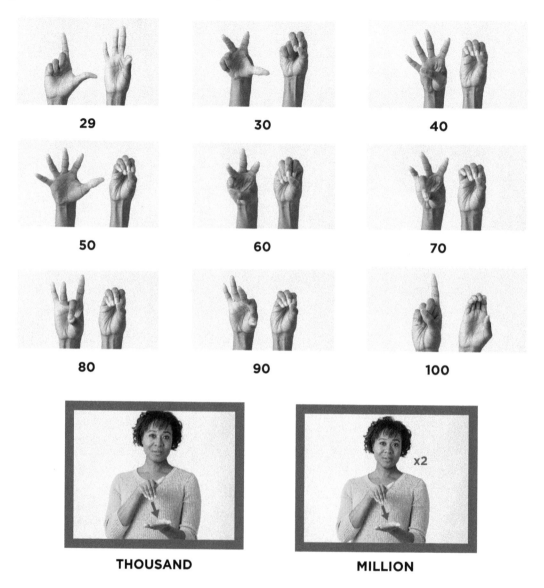

29

30

40

50

60

70

80

90

100

THOUSAND

MILLION

Day 3: I Am . . .

Introductions are a major part of Deaf culture, so learning to introduce yourself in ASL is very important. Today, you will learn a basic introduction to get you started, including signing and fingerspelling your name, indicating age, and telling whether you are Deaf or Hearing.

My name is _____.

MY

NAME IS ...

MY: Your dominant hand is in the flat B handshape. Place it on your chest, just under the collarbone.

NAME: Both hands are in the H handshape. Hold both hands horizontally, forming an X shape with your dominant hand on top of the non-dominant hand's fingers. Tap the dominant hand twice.

[Your name]: After you have signed NAME, fingerspell your name using the ASL alphabet you learned in Day 1. Take your time, be smooth, keep your hand still (no bouncing or knocking), and aim for accuracy over speed.

Memory Tip: The X shape you place your H hand in to form the sign resembles the sign after the X on a signature line.

I am hearing.

I

HEARING

I: Point to yourself, touching your chest, with your dominant hand in the 1 handshape.

HEARING: The dominant hand is in the 1 handshape, with the finger held horizontally in front of the lips. Circle the finger out away from the lips twice.

> **Memory Tip:** The finger circles out from your mouth as if words were spilling out of your mouth from talking.

I am _____ years old.

I

AGE

I: Point to yourself, touching your chest, with your dominant hand in the 1 handshape.

AGE: The dominant hand starts in a tight C handshape at the chin, with the chin slightly inside the hold the hand makes around it. Pull the hand downward and squeeze the hand closed to end in an S handshape.

How to sign AGE, or how many years, months, or days a person has been alive: You will sign OLD, and in one fluid movement from the ending S handshape, curve the hand up and in front of your body and then sign the number of your age. Use the number you learned from Day 2.

Memory Tip: This sign shows you pulling down your long beard, as if you were an old wizard.

Related Vocabulary

YOU: The dominant hand is in the 1 hand-shape. Point toward the person you are referring to.

HARD OF HEARING: Holding the dominant hand in the H handshape and in front of the body, tap the H once. Make a small arch and move it out and away, and tap one more time.

Memory Tip: The H taps down and then taps again, with two Hs representing each word in the phrase.

DEAF: The dominant hand is in the 1 hand-shape with the palm facing out. Tap the fingertip at the side of the chin, and then arch back and tap in front of the ear on the cheek. You will also see this signed from the ear to the chin.

Memory Tip: The tapping at the corner of the mouth and near the ear refers to the person not being able to speak or to hear. While this may be the origin of the sign, being Deaf does not mean that you cannot speak.

Activity

Practice introducing yourself by first signing MY NAME and then fingerspell your name. Sign your age and your hearing status by signing I AGE and the number and then I and either DEAF, HARD OF HEARING, or HEARING. Do this a few times until you feel comfortable.

Day 4: Greetings

Hello, it's nice to meet you.

HELLO

NICE

MEET-you

HELLO: Your dominant hand is in the open B handshape. Place the side of the index finger to the side of the forehead, and bring your hand up and out as if saluting.

NICE: Both hands are in the open B handshape. Your non-dominant hand is palm up, held in front of your body, and your dominant hand, palm down, slides from the base of the palm to the fingertips.

MEET-you: Both hands are in the 1 handshape. Your non-dominant hand is facing in, and your dominant hand is facing out. They start apart from one another and come together with the knuckles of both hands touching.

Memory Tip: MEET-you shows two people walking up to one another.

See you later.

SEE-you LATER

SEE-you LATER: While this sign is technically two separate signs, you blend them together. Sign SEE, and as you pull your hand forward, twist your hand around into the L handshape, and finish with the movement for the sign LATER.

Memory Tip: You are seeing the person later. Later shows that it's in the future at some point in time.

Related Vocabulary

THANK YOU: Your dominant hand is in the open B handshape, palm in. Start with your fingertips on your chin, and move your hand down to a 45-degree angle.

> **Memory Tip:** It looks like you're blowing someone a kiss.

YOU'RE WELCOME: Both of your hands are in the F handshape, palms out, and held up in front of your shoulders. Shake your hands side to side while buzzing your lips. Other meanings: NO PROBLEM or IT'S NOTHING.

> **Memory Tip:** It's like saying, "Hey, it's no big deal." In English gestures, typically the F handshape held up means "okay." If you have both of them up and are shaking them, you're saying it's okay over and over again.

Activity

Practice your introduction, alternating between Person A and Person B. Repeat this several times until it comes to feel more natural. Which one tends to be easier to sign? Don't forget to rely on the mirror to aid you through this early signing activity.

Person A: Hello, it's nice to meet you.

Person B: I'm [fs your name].

Day 5: I Am Learning

As you begin to learn ASL, you might be nervous to sign with others. In today's lesson, you'll learn how to let people know that you're new to sign language and ask them to please sign slowly. Rest assured that they will be kind and gentle with you.

I am learning ASL.

ASL

I

LEARN

ASL: You will fingerspell the three letters —A-S-L—but you want to do so in one smooth motion, with the L coming out in a flicking motion.

I: Point to yourself, touching your chest, with your dominant hand in the 1 handshape.

LEARN: The non-dominant hand is in the flat B handshape, and the dominant hand starts in the open B handshape. Place them palm to palm, with your dominant hand on top. Pull your dominant hand up, bringing it to your forehead. As you pull your hand up, change the handshape into the flat O. Your hand will end with the fingertips on the forehead.

SIGN

SLOW

PLEASE

SIGN: Both hands are in the 1 handshape, held in front of your body with the fingers pointing toward one another, with the hands held at a 45-degree angle. Circle your fingers toward your body in an alternating pattern.

SLOW: Both hands are in the 5 handshape. Place your dominant hand on top of your non-dominant hand. Drag the hand up until your fingertips are near the wrist of your non-dominant hand. This motion is done somewhat slowly. To demonstrate the degree of slowness, slow down the movement.

> **Memory Tip:** When you sign SLOW, your top hand slides up the bottom hand, moving in a slow caress.

PLEASE: Your dominant hand is in the open B handshape. Place it on your chest, underneath your collarbone, and circle your hand starting in a downward motion.

Related Vocabulary

NEW: The non-dominant hand is in the open B handshape, and the dominant hand is in the bent B handshape. Using your dominant hand, make a scooping motion on the palm of your non-dominant hand, leading with the fingertips and going in the direction of the length of your non-dominant hand.

Memory Tip: The scooping of your dominant hand is similar to that satisfying first scoop out of a new jar of peanut butter or, even better, an ice cream container. Other meaning: FRESH.

HELP: The non-dominant hand is in the open B handshape, and the dominant hand is in the open A handshape. With your non-dominant palm facing up in front of your body, you place your dominant hand on the palm, in the thumbs-up position. Raise your non-dominant hand twice.

Memory Tip: Your bottom hand lifts up your top hand—providing support and help, doing the movement for the other hand.

WANT: Both hands are in the bent 5 hand-shape, with palms up and in front of the body. Pull your hands toward your body.

Memory Tip: The movement resembles pulling a drawer open.

START: The non-dominant hand is in the 5 handshape with the dominant hand in the 1 handshape. Place the index finger in the webbing between the index and middle finger of the non-dominant hand. Twist your fingers outward once. Other meaning: BEGIN.

Memory Tip: The twisting looks like starting your car, with your finger representing your keys.

Activity

Yesterday, you practiced your introduction. Today you'll learn to add that you are a new signer. Practice your mini introduction again, and after you sign your name and hearing status, add ASL I LEARN. Consider adding the phrase SIGN SLOW PLEASE.

Day 6: Questions

Time: 8–10 minutes

Questions are an important part of everyday conversation and connection. Today, you'll learn some of the most common question signs. But first, some background: Clarity is always the objective in ASL. As you sign long conversations with others, you need to be able to track what is communicated.

In written English, we use punctuation and grammar rules to alert our readers that we're asking a question. When we speak English, we use inflection, tone, and other cues to let our listeners know that we're asking them a question. It is the same in ASL. We place the question sign at the end of the sentence so that others know they are being asked a question. We use our facial expressions in place of a question mark or inflection to indicate that we're asking a question. Without these cues, we would not be asking a question and our communications would no longer be accurate.

The importance of facial expressions in ASL cannot be overstated. You'll use expressions to show that you're asking a question, to demonstrate the feeling of the message you're expressing, and to give clarity to your signs. For yes/no questions, you raise your eyebrows and tilt your head forward. Furrow your eyebrows and tilt your head for WH-questions—WHO, WHAT, WHEN, WHERE, and WHY—or any question that cannot be answered with a "yes" or a "no."

As you work through this lesson, try practicing facial expressions that go along with questions and then adding their matching sign.

THAT

WHAT?

THAT: There is both a generic and a specific way to sign THAT. For the general way, your dominant hand is in the Y handshape, and your non-dominant hand is in the flat B handshape, palm up. Place the Y hand into the palm of your non-dominant hand. Only use your dominant hand and aim your palm in the direction of the subject you're referring to when signing THAT to refer to a specific object. Your palm starts out and ends palm down. Just point your hand in the direction of any person or object before signing WOMAN, CAR, LAMP, DOG, and so on. For instance, if you're in a room with multiple lamps and you're discussing a specific lamp, aim your hand toward that one. If it's too hard to aim your hand toward a specific person or object or it's not near you, use the general version of this sign.

WHAT: Both hands are in the bent 5 handshape, palms facing up. Shake your hands side to side and furrow your eyebrows while bending your hand forward.

Memory Tip: The sign for WHAT is rather intuitive. If someone gives you a funny look or says something from across the room that you can't understand, you throw your hands out in confusion.

Where do you work?

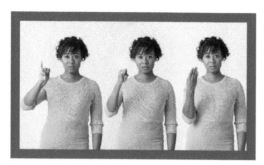

JOB

WHERE?

JOB: JOB is a lexicalized sign, meaning it involves fingerspelling in a specific way that has become a sign rather than just a string of letters. To sign JOB, first sign J, and as you curve your hand in the J shape, flick your hand out into the B handshape with the palm facing toward yourself.

WHERE: Hold your dominant hand up, in the 1 handshape, palm out. Shake your finger side to side while furrowing your eyebrows and tilting your head.

> **Memory Tip:** When you sign WHERE, you move your pointer finger side to side, as if asking, "Is it over there, or is it over there?"

How many?

HOW-MANY

HOW-MANY: This sign specifically asks "how many" or "how much." Start with both hands in the S handshape, palms up and in front of the body. Open the hands upward into the loose 5 handshape. You need to furrow your eyebrows while signing this question.

Memory Tip: You're throwing your fingers up in the air, as if trying to count how many objects were in your hands.

Related Vocabulary

WHEN: Both hands are in the 1 handshape, with your non-dominant hand in front of the body, palm facing the side. Your dominant hand is palm down, with the tip of your finger a few inches above your non-dominant hand. Circle your finger around and down, ending with your fingertips touching.

Memory Tip: Your top hand is circling around as if you were searching for a specific date on your calendar with your finger. The shape you're drawing in the air is similar to a question mark. Circle around, and then make a short line down.

HOW: You use this sign when asking, "In what way or manner?" or about the condition or quality of something: "How does it work?" or "How was your vacation?" Both hands are in the bent B handshape, knuckles together and palms facing in. Twist your dominant wrist to end with your palm up. Your eyebrows should be furrowed, with your head leaned forward slightly.

Memory Tip: Your hand tips forward as if you are asking for evidence or an explanation.

Activity

Play with the phrases from previous lessons by adding a WH-question sign to the end of each one. For example, ASL I LEARN HOW? How do I learn ASL? Try to pick the best question sign for each phrase, but don't worry if it makes sense. The point of this activity is for you to remember the sign, its placement, and the facial expression.

Day 7: Answers

The ability to answer questions is crucial to a meaningful conversation, so today's lesson teaches you a few possible helpful responses. While each of the signs from today's lesson has a specific meaning, you can easily change it with your facial expression and body language. For example, UNDERSTAND can change from the affirmative to the negative by simply adding a negative facial expression and shaking your head "no."

Try playing with each sign from today's lesson, using a few different facial expressions. Positive, affirmative facial expressions include raising your eyebrows, nodding your head, and smiling. Negative facial expressions include furrowing your brow, pursing your lips, shaking your head, and frowning. Your facial expressions and body can show sarcasm, confusion, and more.

Yes, I am fine.

YES

I

FINE

YES: Your dominant hand is in the S hand-shape, palm down, in front of the body. Bend your wrist up and down.

> **Memory Tip:** When you sign YES, your hand represents your head nodding up and down in agreement.

I: Point to yourself, touching your chest, with your dominant hand in the 1 handshape.

FINE: Your dominant hand is in the 5 hand-shape with your palm facing the side. Bring your thumb to your chest.

I understand.

I

UNDERSTAND

I: Point to yourself, touching your chest, with your dominant hand in the 1 handshape.

UNDERSTAND: Your dominant hand is in the 1 handshape, palm facing in and held up near your forehead at the side of your head. Flick your index finger up twice.

> **Memory Tip:** This refers to the light bulb going on when you finally understand something or have a good idea.

Related Vocabulary

RIGHT: Both hands are in the 1 handshape, hands held horizontally and at a diagonal angle in front of the body. Tap the fist of the dominant hand on top of the non-dominant hand. Other meaning: CORRECT.

Memory Tip: Your hands are in the same shape, and you're bringing them together to show that they match perfectly.

KNOW: Your dominant hand is in the flat B handshape. Tap the side of your forehead at the temple. You may often see this sign tapping the cheekbone for efficiency. Both are correct forms of the sign. Other meaning: KNOWLEDGE.

Memory Tip: This sign references the information you have stored in your brain.

NOT: The dominant hand is in the open A handshape, palm facing the side. Place the thumb under the chin and bring it forward, away from your body, in a swift movement. Other meaning: DON'T.

Memory Tip: Many of the negative signs push away from the body, as if distancing the signer from the unwanted object.

Activity

Play with your facial expressions when you sign each of today's vocabulary words. Sign each one showing excitement, contentment, and boredom. You can show the opposite meaning by signing UNDERSTAND, RIGHT, KNOW, and FINE by shaking your head and showing a negative facial expression. Signing it this way now means you don't understand, wrong, you don't know, and you aren't fine. Facial expressions are powerful.

Day 8: Reactions

Time: 15–18 minutes

In today's lesson, you'll learn more vocabulary that will be helpful when you want to respond to various types of inquiries. As you are working on today's lesson, be sure to incorporate a range of facial expressions. Try signing each word several times using a different emotion. For instance, with SORRY, you can sign it as if you were embarrassed, begging for forgiveness, sarcastic, unsure, or frustrated. Go through each sign and think of all the ways you've said those words in real life, identify the range of emotions, and then sign them showing those same emotions on your face and in the way you sign.

I feel nervous.

I

NERVOUS

FEEL

I: Your dominant hand is in the 1 handshape. Touch the middle of your chest with your fingertip.

NERVOUS: Both hands are in the 5 hand-shape, palms down, and in front of your body. Shake your hands as if you were very jittery.

Memory Tip: When you sign NERVOUS, your hands are shaking as though you had one too many cups of coffee.

FEEL: Your dominant hand is in the 5 hand-shape with the middle finger extended forward. Your palm is facing in. Brush your hand up your chest in a circular motion, twice. You are making contact with your chest with your extended middle finger only.

I don't like travel.

TRAVEL

I

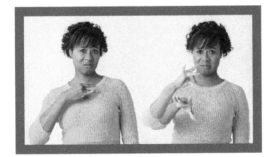

DON'T-LIKE

TRAVEL: Your dominant hand is in the bent 2 handshape, palm down. Move your hand out and away from yourself in a counter-clockwise circle.

Memory Tip: TRAVEL is showing you moving from spot to spot around a map.

I: Your dominant hand is in the 1 handshape. Touch the middle of your chest with your fingertip.

DON'T-LIKE: Start with your dominant hand in the 5 handshape, against your chest. Pull your hand out, as if pulling a string, and as you pull, bring your thumb and middle fingers together in the middle. This is the sign for LIKE. To make it mean DON'T-LIKE, once you've pulled your fingers out a few inches, turn your wrist out and flick your middle finger off your thumb, as if you were flicking a piece of lint off your shirt.

Related Vocabulary

SORRY: Your dominant hand is in the S handshape. Place it on your chest and move it in a circle toward your non-dominant side.

Memory Tip: "S" stands for sorry, near your heart, as though apologizing from the heart.

SURE: Your dominant hand is in the 1 hand-shape palm to the side. Start the sign with the side of your fingertip on your chin. Slide your hand up and out in an arch. Use matching facial expressions, nonchalance, excitement, or whatever best matches your use. Other meanings: TRUE or REALLY.

Memory Tip: When you sign SURE, your finger is showing the affirming word coming out of your mouth.

STRESS: Your non-dominant hand is in the S handshape, palm facing the side. Your dominant hand is in the 5 handshape and is on top of the S handshape. Push your S hand downward twice with your 5 hand.

Memory Tip: You're showing a bottle being pressurized again and again that will explode at any minute.

Activity

Use the signs from the word bank to fill in the blanks of these sentences. (The "answer" is up to you!) Sign each sentence using your facial expressions. Do this one to three times per sentence.

YESTERDAY _____ I FEEL
BROTHER HE _____
US-TWO _____ WHAT? WORK

WORD BANK:			
FINE	SURE	SORRY	STRESS
AWESOME	NERVOUS	DON'T-LIKE	HAPPY
UPSET		ENJOY	SUCCESS

Day 9: Family and Friends

It's time to start adding more depth to your vocabulary. In today's lesson, you'll learn signs for some of the most important people in your life.

I have three sisters and one brother.

3	**SISTER**
1	**BROTHER**
I	**HAVE**

SISTER: The non-dominant hand begins in the A handshape, while the dominant hand is in the open A handshape. Hold the non-dominant hand in front of the body while placing the dominant hand's thumb on the cheek, near the mouth. Bring your dominant hand down on top of the non-dominant hand. As you do this movement, both hands change into the 1 handshape.

BROTHER: The non-dominant hand begins in the A handshape, while the dominant hand is in the open A handshape. Hold the non-dominant hand in front of the body, with the dominant hand's thumb on the side of the forehead. Bring your dominant hand down on top of the non-dominant hand. As you do this movement, *both hands* change into the 1 handshape.

Memory Tip: SISTER and BROTHER are abbreviations of the signs BOY/GIRL and SAME (meaning "from the same family").

I: Point to yourself, touching your chest, with your dominant hand in the 1 handshape.

HAVE: Both hands are in the bent B handshape. Bring the fingertips to the sides of your chest, right where suspenders would go in a firm movement.

I will visit my family soon.

SOON

MY

FAMILY

I

VISIT

SOON: Your dominant hand is in the F hand-shape, palm facing in, with your hand held horizontally. Place the circled fingers on your chin, just underneath your bottom lip. Your mouth is in a pursed O shape, as if you were blowing out your candles.

MY: With the dominant hand in the flat B handshape, place it on your chest, just under the collarbone.

FAMILY: Both hands are in the F handshape, palms out, with the tips of your thumbs and index fingers together in front of your body. Circle your hands around to have your pinkies touch, with your palms facing in.

I: Point to yourself, touching your chest, with your dominant hand in the 1 handshape.

VISIT: Both hands are in the 2 handshape with your palms facing in and hands held in front of the body. Circle your hands in small to medium-size circles, in an alternating motion, toward your body two times.

DAUGHTER

SON

SHE

HAVE

DAUGHTER: Both hands are in the flat B handshape. Your non-dominant hand is palm up in front of your body, as if holding a baby. Start with the dominant hand touching the side of the chin with the side of your index finger, palm down. Bring the dominant hand down on top of the non-dominant arm, landing palm up.

SON: Both hands are in the flat B handshape. Your non-dominant hand is palm up in front of your body, as if holding a baby. Start with the dominant hand touching the side of the forehead with the side of your index finger, palm down. Bring the dominant hand down on top of the non-dominant arm, landing palm up.

Memory Tip: DAUGHTER and SON are combinations of the sign BOY/GIRL and BABY.

SHE: Point off to the side with your dominant hand in the 1 handshape. You can point in a specific direction, if one applies. If it's a general use of the sign, point to the side of your dominant hand.

HAVE or HAS: Both hands are in the bent B handshape. Bring the fingertips to the sides of your chest, right where suspenders would go, in a firm movement. Note: ASL does not have a tense variation for HAVE and HAS. If you would say "had" in English, you'd sign HAVE in ASL.

Related Vocabulary

MOM: Your dominant hand is in the 5 hand-shape, palm facing the side. Place your thumb on the side of your chin, just under the corner of your mouth on your dominant hand's side.

Memory Tip: Signs related to women are signed around the chin.

DAD: Your dominant hand is in the 5 hand-shape, palm facing the side. Place your thumb on the side of your forehead on your dominant hand's side.

Memory Tip: Signs related to men are signed around the forehead.

FRIEND: Both hands are in the X handshape. Your non-dominant hand is palm up, and your dominant hand is palm down. Hook the index fingers together in this position and then flip the hands so that the dominant hand is now on the bottom. For a female friend, make the sign near the chin; for a male friend, make it near the forehead; and for neutral gender, make it around the ear.

GRANDMA: Start out by signing MOM; then arch your hand out in two small arches away from your chin.

GRANDPA: Start out by signing DAD; then arch your hand out in two small arches away from your forehead.

COUSIN: Your dominant hand is in the C handshape, palm facing the side. Hold the hand near the ear at the side of the head but not touching. Circle the hand twice in small circles. You can move your hand up near your forehead to indicate a male cousin and lower near your jaw to indicate a female cousin. Otherwise, sign it near your ear for the general term cousin.

Activity

Label each person in your family using the appropriate sign for their relationship to you, and then fingerspell their name. For instance, BROTHER T-R-E-N-T. Add your friends and their names for additional fingerspelling practice.

Day 10: Hanging Out!

In today's lesson, you'll learn to invite your friends to hang out in a variety of ways. You'll also practice the days of the week. Let's get to hanging and planning!

I sent the invitation.

INVITE

I

FINISH

SEND

INVITE: Your dominant hand is in the open B handshape, palm up. Hold the hand away from your body, off to your dominant side. Bring the hand in toward your torso. Other meanings: WELCOME or HIRE.

I: Your dominant hand is in the 1 handshape. Touch the middle of your chest with your fingertip.

FINISH: Both hands are in the 5 handshape, palms in, with the hands up in front of the shoulder area. Flip your wrists out toward the sides, ending with your palms out.

SEND: The non-dominant hand is in the open B handshape, palm down and in front of the body. The dominant hand starts in the bent B handshape, with the fingertips on the back of the non-dominant hand. Flick the fingertips off, ending with your dominant hand in the open B handshape.

MOVIE

YOU

WATCH

WANT?

MOVIE: The non-dominant hand is in the flat B handshape, palm facing in, and the dominant hand is in the 5 handshape, palm out. Place the dominant hand behind the non-dominant hand, and shake the dominant hand back and forth.

YOU: The dominant hand is in the 1 handshape. Point toward the person you are referring to.

WATCH: Your dominant hand is in the bent L handshape in front of your body, palm up. Bring the hand forward in a single movement.

Memory Tip: WATCH is signed like you're holding a remote control and aiming it at a receiver.

WANT: Both hands are in the bent 5 handshape, palms up, and in front of the body. Pull your hands toward your body as if opening a drawer.

I will attend her party.

HER

PARTY

I

ATTEND

WILL

HER: Your dominant hand is in the flat B handshape, palm out at a 45-degree angle. Point the palm off to the side. If you're talking about a specific person, point the palm toward that person if they're near you.

PARTY: Both hands are in the Y handshape, arms held horizontally out in front of the body. Move both hands side to side in tandem.

I: Your dominant hand is in the 1 handshape. Touch the middle of your chest with your fingertip.

ATTEND: This is GO signed twice. Start with both hands in the 1 handshape, held vertically, angled to the side of your dominant hand. In a sharp movement, bring them both down at the same time twice, ending with your palms facing the ground.

Memory Tip: ATTEND is signing GO two times—you are go-go-ing somewhere.

WILL: Your dominant hand is in the open B handshape, palm to the side, and held near the head. Arch the hand forward in two small arches. Other meaning: FUTURE.

Is _____ close by?

fs LOCATION

IT

CLOSE-BY?

IT: With your dominant hand in the 1 hand-shape, point to the side. You can point in a specific direction if it applies. If it's a general use of the sign, point off to the side of your dominant hand.

CLOSE-BY: Your dominant hand is in the F handshape and the palm in. With the tip of your circled index and thumb fingers brush them off the tip of your nose in a downward direction. As you do so, hold your mouth in a tight *ooo* shape.

> **Memory Tip:** CLOSE-BY shows that it's so close that you have to look over your nose to see it.

Related Vocabulary

MONDAY: The dominant hand is in the M handshape, palm facing toward you. Circle the M in a counterclockwise motion.

WEDNESDAY: The dominant hand is in the W handshape, palm facing toward you. Circle the W in a counterclockwise motion.

TUESDAY: The dominant hand is in the T handshape, palm facing toward you. Circle the T in a counterclockwise motion twice.

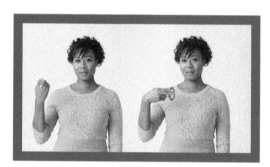

THURSDAY: The dominant hand first forms a T and then shoots out into the H handshape, palm facing toward you. Circle the H in a tiny circle away from your body.

FRIDAY: The dominant hand is in the F handshape, palm facing toward you. Circle the F in a counterclockwise motion.

SUNDAY: Both hands are in the open B handshape. Hold the hands up in front of your body at eye level. Circle both hands in opposite directions. The circles are small.

Memory Tip: Your hands are up as if you were worshiping.

SATURDAY: The dominant hand is in the S handshape, palm facing toward you. Circle the S in a counterclockwise motion.

Memory Tip: Each sign, Monday through Saturday, begins with the first letter of that day of the week.

Activity

Using the first three sentences, add a day of the week in front of the sentence (TIME). Sign each new sentence. Do this one to three times per sentence.

Day 11: Events

Time: 15–20 minutes

Today, you will learn signs for common events and celebrations.

What holiday are you celebrating?

HOLIDAY

YOU

CELEBRATE

WHICH?

HOLIDAY: Both hands are in the 5 handshape. Tap the thumbs onto your chest twice, a few inches from your armpits.

YOU: The dominant hand is in the 1 handshape. Point toward the person you are referring to.

CELEBRATE: Both hands are in the baby O handshape, palms in and hands above the shoulders. Circle your hands around in the air and smile.

WHICH: Both hands are in the open A handshape, palms facing one another. Move the hands up and down in an alternating motion while furrowing the eyebrows.

What are you doing for Spring Break?

SOON

YOU

SPRING

BREAK

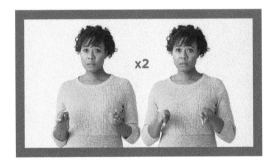

HAPPEN

WHAT-DO?

SOON: Your dominant hand is in the F handshape, palm facing in and hand held horizontally. Place the circled fingers on your chin, just underneath your bottom lip. Your mouth is in a pursed O shape, as if you were blowing out your candles.

YOU: The dominant hand is in the 1 handshape. Point toward the person you are referring to.

SPRING: Your non-dominant hand is in the flat C handshape, palm facing the side. Your dominant hand is in the flat O handshape palm up. Place the fingertips of the flat O hand in the space between the flat C hand. Push your hand up through the opening, and as you do, open the hand into a 5 hand in a cone shape. Repeat this motion one more time.

> **Memory Tip:** Spring is showing a plant growing out of the ground.

BREAK: Your non-dominant hand is in the flat B handshape, palm to the side. Your dominant hand is in the flat B handshape, palm down. Slide the dominant hand between the middle and ring fingers of the non-dominant hand.

HAPPEN: Both hands are in the 1 handshape held horizontally in front of the body with palms facing each other. Twist your wrists to bring the hands down with the palms facing down.

WHAT-DO: Both hands are in the D handshape, palms up. Tap your index finger on your thumb two to three times. While you sign this, your eyebrows are furrowed and your mouth is in the *ooo* shape, as if you were saying "do."

Related Vocabulary

BIRTHDAY: Your dominant hand is in the 5 handshape with the middle finger extended forward. Place the tip of your middle finger on the center of your chin and then bring it down to touch your chest, around your collarbone.

Memory Tip: This is a combination of FAVORITE and pointing to yourself.

BAR/BAT MITZVAH: Both hands are in the S handshape, palms in. Hold the dominant hand over the non-dominant hand, arms horizontal across the body. Circle the hands around each other, ending in the starting position.

FEAST: Both hands are in the flat O handshape. In alternating arching movements, sign EAT without touching the hands to the mouth but toward it.

PARTY: Both hands are in the Y handshape, arms held out horizontally in front of the body. Move both hands side to side in tandem.

Memory Tip: Hands move together in a dance.

WEDDING: Both hands are in the open B handshape, palm facing in. Your hands are in front of your body, with the fingertips angled down and out. In an arching motion bring the hands together, with the dominant hand to overlap over the non-dominant hand.

Memory Tip: Two hands joining together in marriage.

ANNIVERSARY: Both hands are in the baby O handshape, palms in, hands above the shoulders. Circle your hands around in the air and smile. Other meaning: CELEBRATE.

Memory Tip: Twirling flags in the air in celebration.

Activity

Using the time-related signs you've learned so far, combine them with your event signs, putting the time first and then the event—for instance, YESTERDAY BIRTHDAY, WEEKEND ANNIVERSARY. You can be as general or specific as you'd like. For an added challenge, try fingerspelling the name of the month or use the number signs to sign the date.

Day 12: Health and Safety

Time: 15 minutes

In today's lesson, you'll learn signs for your basic safety, illness, and health.

Last night I was sick and throwing up.

PAST

NIGHT

I

SICK

I

THROW-UP

PAST: Your dominant hand is in the open B handshape, palm facing in. Starting in front of your dominant shoulder, move the hand backward toward the space behind you.

NIGHT: The non-dominant hand is in the flat B handshape. Your non-dominant arm is held in front of the body horizontally. The dominant hand is in the bent B handshape. Place the wrist of the dominant hand on top of the non-dominant hand, with the fingertips over the edge, pointing toward the floor.

Memory Tip: When you sign NIGHT, the bottom arm shows the horizon and the top hand shows the position of the sun in relationship to the horizon. In this case, it's under the horizon where you can't see it.

I: Your dominant hand is in the 1 handshape. Touch the middle of your chest with your fingertip.

SICK: Both hands are in the 5 handshape with the middle finger extended forward. Place the tip of your middle finger of your dominant hand on the side of your forehead and the tip of the middle finger of your non-dominant hand on the side of your stomach.

THROW-UP: Both hands are in the 5 handshape with the dominant hand just in front of the mouth, palm facing the side. The non-dominant hand is just in front of the dominant hand. Together arch them forward and down. Your face needs to match the feeling.

I am allergic to nuts.

MYSELF

ALLERGY

NUTS

MYSELF: Your dominant hand is in the open A handshape with the palm facing the side. Tap your chest twice with the back of your thumb.

ALLERGY: This is a two-part sign. The dominant hand is in the 1 handshape and touches the tip of your nose. The next movement both hands are in the G handshape fingertips pointing toward one another. Pull your dominant hand away from the non-dominant hand in the opposite direction. Do both parts of this sign together in a fluid motion.

Memory Tip: ALLERGY is a combination of two signs: NOSE and OPPOSITE.

NUTS: This is very similar to signing NOT, but instead, place the thumb under your two front teeth and pull your open A hand out in a swift movement.

I have a tooth infection and need medicine.

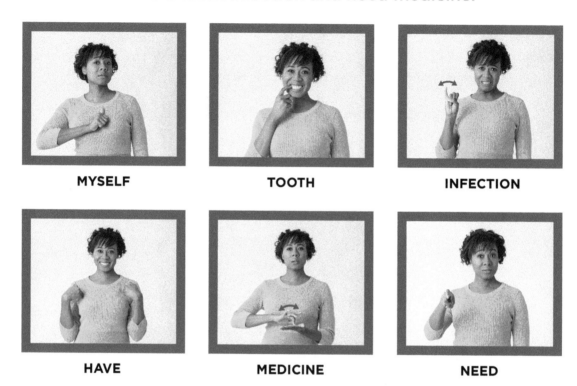

MYSELF　　**TOOTH**　　**INFECTION**

HAVE　　**MEDICINE**　　**NEED**

MYSELF: Your dominant hand is in the open A handshape with the palm facing the side. Tap your chest twice with the back of your thumb.

TOOTH: With your dominant hand in the X handshape, tap your tooth, just to the side of your two front teeth. Other meaning: GLASS (if tapping your front two teeth).

INFECTION: Hold your dominant hand up near your shoulder in the I handshape. Shake the hand side to side. It's very important that you scrunch your face up in a look of disgust; otherwise it will mean INSURANCE, not INFECTION.

HAVE: Both hands are in the bent B handshape. Bring the fingertips to your chest, right where suspenders would go.

MEDICINE: Your non-dominant hand is in the open B handshape, palm up, and your dominant hand is in the 5 handshape. Place the tip of the middle finger in the center of the palm of your open B hand. Wiggle your dominant hand back and forth.

NEED: Your dominant hand is in the X handshape, palm out and in front of your body. Bend your wrist and your palm ends facing down.

I see my awesome nurse at the hospital this afternoon.

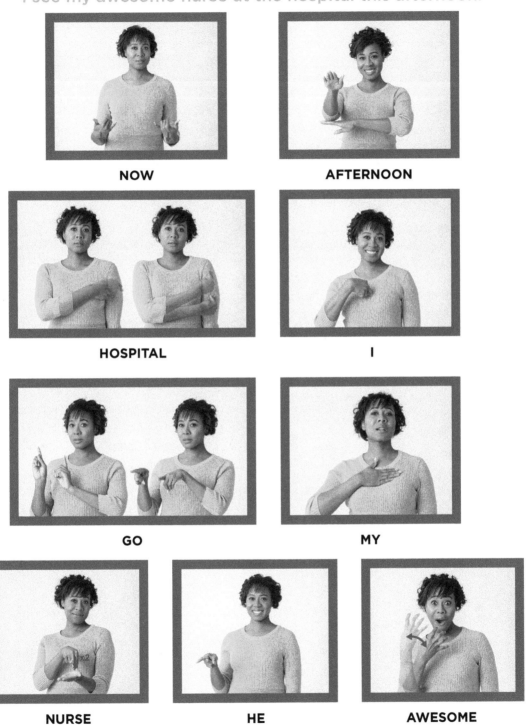

NOW

AFTERNOON

HOSPITAL

I

GO

MY

NURSE

HE

AWESOME

NOW: Both hands are in the Y handshape palms facing up. Bring the hands down quickly one time.

AFTERNOON: Both hands are in the flat B handshape. Your non-dominant arm is held in front of the body horizontally. The forearm of the dominant hand rests on the fingertips of the non-dominant arm, with the dominant arm at a 45-degree angle.

HOSPITAL: With your dominant hand in the H handshape, draw a plus sign on the side of your non-dominant arm.

I: Your dominant hand is in the 1 handshape. Touch the middle of your chest with your fingertip.

GO: Both hands are in the 1 handshape. Start with both hands held vertically, the hands angled to the side of your dominant hand. In a sharp movement, bring them both down at the same time, ending with your palms facing the ground.

MY: Your dominant hand is in the flat B handshape, and you place it on your chest, just under the collarbone.

NURSE: Your non-dominant hand is in the open B handshape and is horizontal with your palm facing out at a 45-degree angle. Your dominant hand is in the U handshape and taps the wrist of your non-dominant hand twice.

Memory Tip: NURSE shows a person taking your pulse.

HE: With your dominant hand in the 1 handshape, point off to the side. You can point in a specific direction if it applies. If it's a general use of the sign, point off to the side of your dominant hand.

AWESOME: Your dominant hand is in the bent 5 handshape, palm facing in. Hold your hand just in front of your mouth and shake your hand side to side. Open your mouth in the "ahhhh" shape.

Related Vocabulary

PAIN: Both of your hands are in the 1 hand-shape, palms in, hands horizontal. Bring the index fingers toward each other while simultaneously twisting in opposite directions. You can place this sign in front of any body part that hurts to show where the pain is or sign this in front of your body to mean pain or hurt in general. Other meaning: HURT.

911: Fingerspell the numbers 9-1-1.

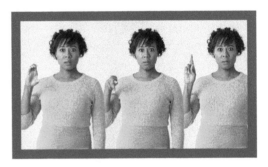

Memory Tip: The fingers touching show the nerves coming together in pain.

CPR: Fingerspell the letters C-P-R.

Note: The sign PAIN can be signed in various locations and mean different things. If you sign PAIN in front of your head, it means headache, and in front of your stomach, stomachache. You can show that your knee, your back, and anywhere else on your body hurts. Practice signing PAIN in 10 different locations on your body. If you can't sign PAIN in front of that body part, point to it first and then sign PAIN. For example, you would point to your wrist and then sign PAIN. You can move your hands in front of your shoulder and sign PAIN and your audience would understand you're signing shoulder pain.

HEART: The dominant hand is in the 5 hand-shape, with the middle finger extended forward. Tap the area above your heart twice with the tip of your middle finger.

STROKE: The dominant hand is in the flat B handshape, and the palm faces the side. Draw a zigzagging line down the front of the body, starting at the forehead. You are just in front of your body, not touching it.

BONE: Both of your hands are in the bent V handshape, palms facing in. Cross your arms over one another and tap the arms together twice.

BREATH: Both hands are in the 5 hand-shape, held horizontally in front of the chest and stomach, with the dominant hand above the non-dominant hand. Move the hands forward, away from the body a few inches, and bring them back down to the chest. This shows the lungs expanding and contracting. To show that someone is short of breath, do this same sign, but do the movement faster and a few more times. Also, open your mouth as if gasping.

TEST: Both hands are in the X handshape, palms out, in front of your shoulders. Bend your index finger into the X handshape, and move the hands downward; then change your hands into the 5 handshape.

Memory Tip: As you drag your hand down, you're showing all the question marks down the page. Other meanings: EXAM or QUIZ.

Activity

Create five sentences where you describe different illnesses using: SHE SICK _____ SHE HAVE. You'll fingerspell the name of the illness in the blank. Do this five times, each time with a different fingerspelled illness.

Day 13: Feelings

Emotions are a large part of our lives. In today's lesson, you'll learn some of the most common signs to describe what you and others feel. When you first learn an emotion sign, be sure to have a matching facial expression. Don't sign ANGRY and look happy or neutral. If you practice the corresponding facial expression while you learn the sign, you'll make signing with emotion more natural. Remember that you can communicate the same way in sign language as you do in English. If you would normally say sarcastically that you're happy, you can sign HAPPY and show sarcasm with your facial expressions. As you gain confidence in your expressions, you can practice signing with facial expressions that conflict with what you're signing.

As you practice today's lesson, try standing in front of a mirror or use your camera on your phone to watch yourself. Sign each of the new feeling signs you'll learn today while practicing your matching facial expressions. Try subtle, extreme, and a few in-between options, and notice the difference.

I cried yesterday because I was upset.

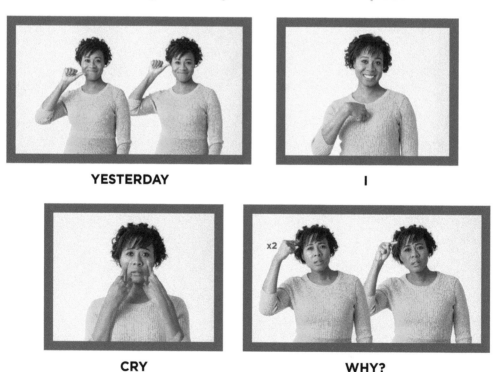

YESTERDAY

I

CRY

WHY?

SAD

UPSET

YESTERDAY: The dominant hand is in the open A handshape. The palm is facing forward, and the thumb is at the side of the chin, close to the cheek. Tap this spot, and in an arching movement, tap the upper cheek near the ear.

I: Point to yourself, touching your chest, with your dominant hand in the 1 handshape.

CRY: Both of your hands are in the 1 handshape, palms facing in. Your fingertips are just under the eyes, and you draw a line down both cheeks twice to show tears dripping down your face.

WHY: Your dominant hand is in the extended 5 handshape, meaning your middle finger is pushed forward. Hold the hand up at the side of your head near your forehead, palm facing your head. Wiggle your middle finger up and down. Furrow your eyebrows, and tilt your head forward. When WHY is signed in the middle of a sentence, like this, raise instead of furrowing your eyebrows.

SAD: Both hands are in the 5 handshape, palms facing in, hands starting just underneath the eyes. Bring the hands straight down the face, ending at the jawline. Your facial expressions are sad.

Memory Tip: CRY shows tears dripping down your cheeks in tracks.

UPSET: Your dominant hand is in the open B handshape palm down, with the side of your thumb and hand resting on your stomach. Flip your hand over, and end with your palm up and the edge of your pinky on your stomach. As you sign this, pull the corners of your mouth down.

Memory Tip: UPSET is signed to show your stomach flipping in discomfort.

You look upset. Are you worried or angry?

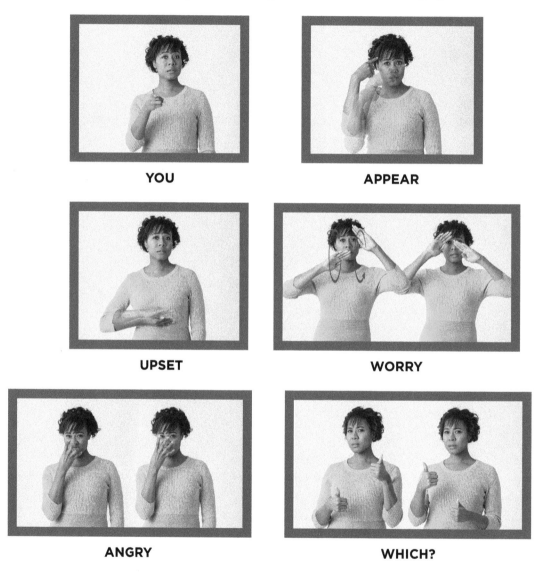

YOU

APPEAR

UPSET

WORRY

ANGRY

WHICH?

YOU: The dominant hand is in the 1 hand-shape. Point toward the person you are referring to.

APPEAR: Your dominant hand is in the 1 handshape. With the tip of your finger, palm facing in, trace a circle around your face. You're not touching your face but just in front of it. Other meaning: LOOK (the adjective).

UPSET: Your dominant hand is in the open B handshape palm down with the side of your thumb and hand resting on your stomach. Flip your hand over and end with your palm up and the edge of your pinky on your stomach. As you sign this, pull the corners of your mouth down.

WORRY: Both of your hands are in the flat B handshape, palms out, and hands in the space in front of your forehead. In alternating circles, circle your hands down and back up two times.

ANGRY: Your dominant hand is in the 5 handshape in front of your face, palm in. Bend your hands into the 5 claw handshape two times. Look angry. Other meaning: MAD.

WHICH: Both hands are in the open A hand-shape, palms facing one another. Move the hands up and down in an alternating motion while furrowing the eyebrows.

I'm excited to graduate this month!

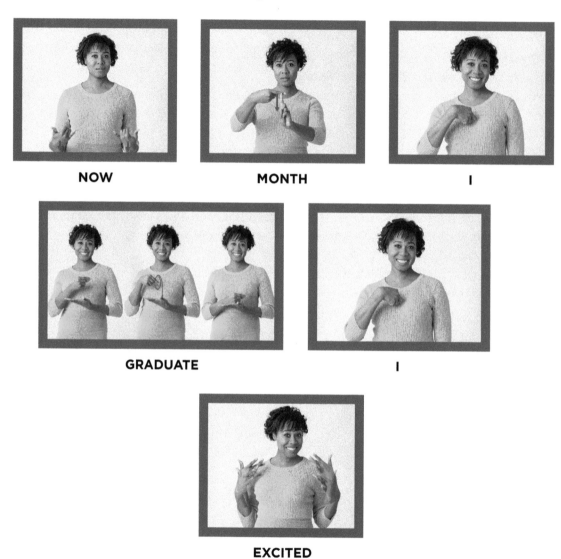

NOW
MONTH
I

GRADUATE
I

EXCITED

NOW: Both hands are in the Y handshape palms facing up, except you bring the hands down quickly and only once.

MONTH: Both hands are in the 1 handshape. Your non-dominant hand is vertical and palm facing out. The dominant hand is horizontal and palm facing you. In a downward movement, drag the dominant hand down the non-dominant hand.

GRADUATE: Hold your non-dominant hand in the open B handshape, palm up and in front of your body. Your dominant hand is in the G handshape above your other hand, palm facing down. Flip your hand over, and land in the middle of your palm with your fist in the palm and your dominant hand's palm facing the side.

I: Point to yourself, touching your chest, with your dominant hand in the 1 handshape.

EXCITED: Both hands are in the 5 handshape with the middle finger extended forward, palms facing in. Alternating between hands, brush your hands up the sides of your chest in a circular motion twice. You are making contact with your chest with your extended middle finger only. Other meaning: THRILLED.

Memory Tip: Lots of happy feelings jumping around in your body.

My new book is wonderful!

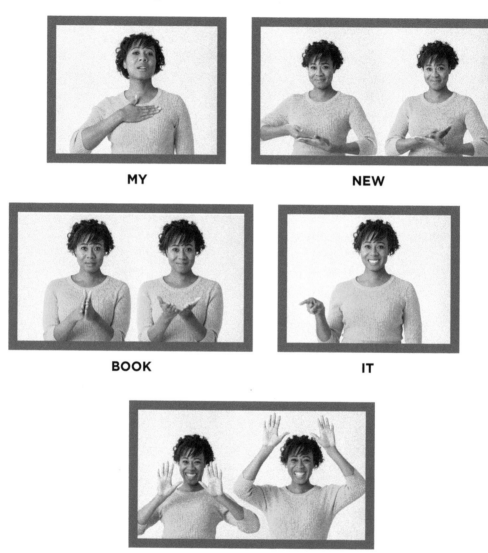

MY

NEW

BOOK

IT

WONDERFUL

MY: Your dominant hand is in the flat B handshape, and you place it on your chest, just under the collarbone.

NEW: The non-dominant hand is in the open B handshape, and the dominant hand is in the bent B handshape. Using your dominant hand, make a scooping motion on the palm of your non-dominant hand, leading with the fingertips and going in the direction of the length of your non-dominant hand.

BOOK: Both of your hands are in the open B handshape with the edges of your pinkies together in the middle. Your hands are forming the front and back covers of the book. Open and close your hands twice.

> **Memory Tip:** BOOK shows you opening and closing a book.

IT: With your dominant hand in the 1 handshape, point off to the side. You can point in a specific direction if it applies. If it's a general use of the sign, point off to the side of your dominant hand.

WONDERFUL: Both hands are in the open B handshape, palms out, hands above the shoulders. Tap the air in front of your hands, and then tap the air in front of your hands again but a few inches lower. Other meaning: GREAT.

Related Vocabulary

HAPPY: Your dominant hand is in the open B handshape, palm in. Brush your hand up your chest in a circular motion twice. As you sign HAPPY, smile or look happy.

Memory Tip: The sign represents the feeling of joy bursting from your chest. Other meaning: JOY.

NEAT: Your dominant hand is in the X handshape, held on the cheek near the side of the mouth. Twist your wrist forward once.

Memory Tip: The movement represents a dimple that shows in your cheek when you grin.

Activity

Use the sentences from today's lesson and the vocabulary from the previous days to create new Mad Lib sentences. If you're changing a question sign in a sentence, be sure to put a different question sign rather than a non-question sign. If it's a feeling sign, use a different feeling sign. For example, in the sentence: MY NEW BOOK IT WONDERFUL, the sign for "wonderful" is an emotion sign. Switch out WONDERFUL with SAD, and you've got a new sentence. You can do the same with BOOK. What other topics can you sign in its place? GOAL, LUNCH, HOME, TABLE, etc.

Day 14: Weather

Time: 15 minutes

Weather is an everyday occurrence and an important part of our lives. Knowing how to sign with others about weather is a great conversational skill. Make note of the types of weather you most talk about with your family and friends. Be sure to practice those signs until they're second nature.

This winter is cold!

NOW

WINTER

IT

COLD

NOW: Both hands are in the Y handshape palms facing up. Bring the hands down quickly one time.

WINTER: Both hands are in the W handshape; with the palms facing in, shake your hands side to side.

IT: With your dominant hand in the 1 handshape, point off to the side. You can point in a specific direction if it applies. If it's a general use of the sign, point off to the side of your dominant hand.

COLD: Both hands are in the S handshape, held out in front of your body, palms facing toward each other. Shake your hands side to side, and have your mouth in the ooo position, as if you are blowing out your birthday candles.

There was a tornado last week.

LAST-WEEK

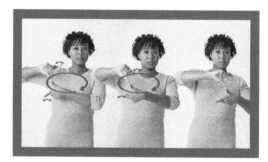

TORNADO

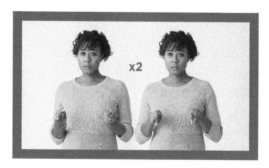

HAPPEN

LAST-WEEK: The non-dominant hand is in the flat B handshape and the dominant hand is in the 1 handshape. Hold the non-dominant hand palm up and in front of the body. Start with your dominant hand palm down at the heel of the non-dominant hand. Bring your hand down the palm toward the fingertips. As you reach the fingertips, bring your dominant hand back toward your shoulder, and twist the palm to face your body.

TORNADO: Both hands are in the L handshape with the thumbs extended. Your non-dominant hand is palm in, and your dominant hand is palm out. Bring the thumb tips together in front of your body with the hands horizontal. Bend your index fingers twice, and move hands in a circle while signing.

Memory Tip: TORNADO shows a twister spinning in place and around the land.

HAPPEN: Both hands are in the 1 handshape held horizontally in front of the body with palms facing each other. Twist your wrists to bring the hands down with the palms facing down. Repeat this movement twice.

SNOW

IT

SCARE

ME

SNOW: Hold both of your 5 hands up in the air near your head. Flutter your fingers as you move your hands down and side to side.

IT: With your dominant hand in the 1 handshape, point off to the side. You can point in a specific direction if it applies. If it's a general use of the sign, point off to the side of your dominant hand.

SCARE: Both of your hands begin in the S handshape, palms facing the body and hands horizontal. Move your hands in toward one another, and as you do, open both hands into the 5 handshape. Open your mouth in a wide O shape as you sign SCARE.

Memory Tip: The movements show your reaction when you get scared—you freeze, and your mouth opens.

ME: Point to yourself, touching your chest, with your dominant hand in the 1 handshape.

It looks really cloudy and windy, but I don't know if we'll get rain.

RAIN

WILL?

DON'T-KNOW

TRUE

APPEAR

CLOUD

WIND

RAIN: Both hands are in the 5 handshape, palms out. Bend your wrist and bring your hands down so that your hands are lower and your palms are down. Repeat this motion one more time.

WILL: Your dominant hand is in the open B handshape, palm facing the side. Hold your hand up above your shoulder by your head. Arch the hand up and forward with your hand ending horizontal. Other meanings: FUTURE or WILL (as a question).

DON'T-KNOW: Your dominant hand is in the flat B handshape. Touch the side of your forehead at the temple and then twist your hand away from your head so that your palm is now facing out.

TRUE: Your dominant hand is in the 1 hand-shape palm to the side. Start the sign with the side of your fingertip on your chin. Slide your hand up and out in an arch.

APPEAR: Your dominant hand is in the 1 handshape. With the tip of your finger, palm facing in, trace a circle around your face. You're not touching your face but just in front of it.

CLOUD: Both hands are in the bent 5 hand-shape, hands up above your head with your non-dominant hand slightly lower than your dominant hand. Your non-dominant hand is palm out, and your dominant hand is palm in. Make alternating circles in the air with both hands.

WIND: Both hands are in the 5 handshape, palms facing each other. Move your arms from the elbow side to side.

> **Memory Tip:** The weather signs, like WIND, show what those conditions look like.

Related Vocabulary

SUMMER: Your dominant hand starts in the 1 handshape, palm down held in front of your forehead. Pull your hand across your forehead, and as you pull it across, change into the X handshape..

SEASON: Your non-dominant hand is in the open B handshape, with the palm facing the side. Your dominant hand is in the S handshape, with the palm facing out. Place the S on the palm of your other hand and circle your hand on the palm once.

EARTH: Your non-dominant hand is in the S handshape and your dominant hand in the open 8 handshape. Place the tips of your middle finger and thumb on the back of your S hand and wiggle the hand forward and back.

Activity

Go on a picture hunt, looking at different images to show a variety of weather conditions. As you identify the various types of weather that match your vocabulary, sign them.

Day 15: Money

In today's lesson, you'll learn how to use the most important signs for money.

My lunch costs $_____.

MY

LUNCH

IT

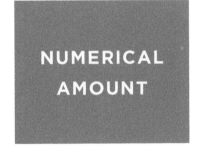

NUMERICAL AMOUNT

MY: Your dominant hand is in the flat B handshape placed on your chest.

LUNCH: First sign EAT with the flat O handshape brought to your lips once. Sign this once and quickly sign NOON. Both hands are in the flat B handshape. Your non-dominant arm is held in front of the body horizontally. Place the elbow on top of the fingertips of the non-dominant hand. Your dominant arm should be vertical with the fingertips pointed up.

Memory Tip: Lunch is a combination sign. You sign it by first signing EAT and then NOON.

IT: With your dominant hand in the 1 handshape, point off to the side. You can point in a specific direction if it applies. If it's a general use of the sign, point off to the side of your dominant hand.

I need my paycheck so I can buy a plane ticket!

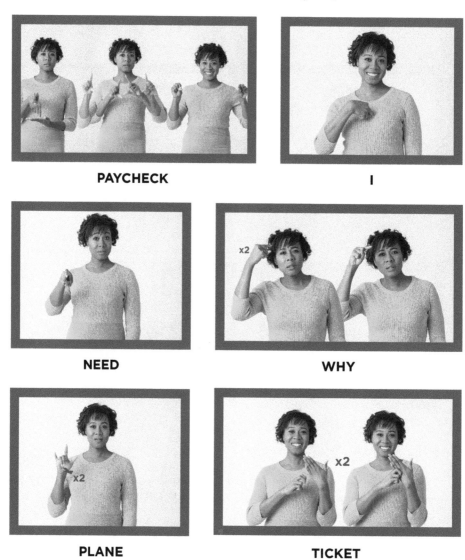

PAYCHECK

I

NEED

WHY

PLANE

TICKET

PAYCHECK: This is a combination sign of PAY and then showing the shape of a check. First sign PAY with your non-dominant hand in the open B handshape and your dominant hand in the 1 handshape, fingertip in the middle of your non-dominant hand's palm. Flick the finger forward and off the palm. Then both hands move to the bent L handshapes. They begin together with the sides of your index fingers and thumbs touching and then move your hands out to show the edges of a check and then pinch each index finger and thumb together to show the short edges of the check.

I: Point to yourself, touching your chest, with your dominant hand in the 1 handshape.

NEED: Your dominant hand is in the X handshape palm out and in front of your body. Bend your wrist and your palm ends facing down.

WHY: Your dominant hand is in the extended 5 handshape, meaning your middle finger is pushed forward. Hold the hand up at the side of your head, near your forehead, palm facing your head. Wiggle your middle finger up and down. Furrow your eyebrows and tilt your head forward. However, when WHY is signed in the middle of a sentence, like this one, you raise your eyebrows instead.

PLANE: Your dominant hand is in the I-L handshape. Your palm is angled down, and your hand is up near your shoulder. Tap your hand forward twice.

TICKET: Your non-dominant hand is in the open B handshape, palm up, and your dominant hand is in the bent 2 handshape, palm in. Move your dominant hand toward your non-dominant hand, sandwiching the edge of your non-dominant hand between the index and middle fingers of your dominant hand.

Memory Tip: TICKET is signed as if a ticket taker was punching a hole in the ticket.

BUY: Your non-dominant hand is in the flat B handshape, and your dominant hand is in the flat O handshape, both palms up. Place the dominant hand on the palm of the non-dominant hand and then move the hand in an arch, forward, as if taking money out of your hand and handing it to the cashier.

Related Vocabulary

BUY: Your non-dominant hand is in the flat B handshape, and your dominant hand is in the flat O handshape, both palms up. Place the dominant hand on the palm of the non-dominant hand, and then move the hand in an arch forward.

> **Memory Tip:** This sign resembles taking money out of your hand and handing it to the cashier.

DOLLAR: Your non-dominant hand is in the open B handshape, palm facing in, and hand held horizontally. Your dominant hand is in the Y handshape but with the pinky finger curled in with the middle three fingers. Place the gap between your bent fingers and palm over your non-dominant hand. Start with the dominant hand nearest the thumb of your non-dominant hand, and then slide your dominant hand across the bottom hand toward the fingertips, stopping just before your hand slides off.

> **Memory Tip:** The bottom hand is the dollar bills, and the top hand is the money clip.

MONEY: Your non-dominant hand is in the flat B handshape, and your dominant hand is in the flat O handshape, both palms up. Tap the dominant hand on the palm of the non-dominant hand twice.

Memory Tip: You are slapping dollar bills against your palm.

PAY: Your non-dominant hand is in the open B handshape, and your dominant hand is in the 1 handshape, fingertip in the middle of your non-dominant hand's palm. Flick the finger forward and off the palm.

Memory Tip: You're pointing to the money in your hand and then at the person you're going to give it to.

Activity

Pull up your favorite online store and find 10 objects you could buy. Sign the prices for each object using the format DOLLAR + the number. Pause for a second after you sign the dollar amount and then sign the cents. You don't need to sign the decimal or CENT.

Day 16: Wellness

Personal health, hygiene, and wellness are parts of our daily lives, and there are countless instances when it's essential to know how to sign about them. You may be chatting with a friend who wants to go out and need to let them know that you need to shower first—or that you're not feeling well so you can't go. Perhaps you need to describe symptoms to a loved one or a doctor. Read on for some common personal health and wellness vocabulary.

You must brush your teeth every day.

DAILY

BRUSH-TEETH

YOU

MUST

DAILY: Your dominant hand is in the open A handshape, palm facing the side. Place the palm side along your cheek and slide it down toward your mouth twice.

BRUSH-TEETH: Your dominant hand is in the 1 handshape, palm down, in front of your mouth. Pull your lips back to expose your teeth. Move your finger up and down and across your teeth at the same time. The up and down motion is very small.

YOU: The dominant hand is in the 1 handshape. Point toward the person you are referring to.

MUST: Your dominant hand is in the X handshape palm out and in front of your body. Bend your wrist and your palm ends facing down. Other meaning: NEED.

Something feels wrong.

SOMETHING

FEEL

WRONG

SOMETHING: Your dominant hand is in the 1 handshape with the palm facing up and the index finger pointed up as well. Circle your hand counterclockwise. This sign has multiple meanings and is dependent on context. Other meanings: SOMEONE, SINGLE, ALONE, or ONLY.

FEEL: Your dominant hand is in the 5 handshape with the middle finger extended forward. Your palm is facing in. Brush your hand up your chest in a circular motion twice. You are making contact with your chest with your extended middle finger only.

Memory Tip: FEEL shows the place where emotions are typically felt: your heart.

WRONG: The dominant hand is in the Y handshape, palm facing in. Place the three bent fingers on your chin, and shake your head slightly in the negative.

Related Vocabulary

HEALTH: Both hands are in a loose bent 5 handshape, palms in, right in front of your shoulders. Pull your hands out, away from your body. As you do, close your hands into the S handshape.

> **Memory Tip:** You're showing your strength, as if flexing your muscles.

SHOWER: Your dominant hand starts in the O handshape to the side and above your head. You open your hand up into the 5 hand, with the thumb under the four fingers to form a cone. Repeat this motion twice.

> **Memory Tip:** It's as if the water is coming out of the shower head.

MENSTRUATE: The dominant hand is in the A handshape and taps the cheek twice.

> **Memory Tip:** This is often signed with the head turned away from others and even signed with your tongue poking the inside of your cheek out to keep it even more private.

WASH: Both hands are in the A handshape, palms together, with the non-dominant hand underneath the dominant hand. Circle both hands together in opposite directions.

> **Memory Tip:** The motion is as if you're rubbing a washrag on a dish.

Activity

Go on a picture hunt using books, magazines, photo albums, or online resources. As you find a variety of health-related images, point to the picture and sign the sign that best matches.

Day 17: In the Home

Time: 10–15 minutes

Today you'll learn signs to use in and around the home plus a directional verb. While not all verb signs can be signed directionally, we sign some to show the verb being used by one person to affect another.

Where is the bathroom?

BATHROOM

WHERE?

BATHROOM: Your dominant hand is in the T handshape, palm out. Shake your hand side to side. Other meaning: TOILET.

Memory Tip: T stands for toilet.

WHERE: Hold your dominant hand up in the 1 handshape, palm out. Shake your finger side to side while furrowing your eyebrows and tilting your head.

YOUR

ROOM

NICE

YOUR: Your dominant hand is in the flat B handshape. Hold the hand out at a slight angle with the palm pointing toward the person you're referencing.

ROOM: Both hands are in the open B handshape, hands held horizontal and palms both facing you. Your dominant hand is in front of your non-dominant hand. Bend both wrists back at the same time so that now both palms are facing each other. Other meaning: CLEAN (as in the state of cleanliness).

Memory Tip: When you sign ROOM, you are indicating the four walls of a room.

NICE: Both hands are in the open B hand-shape. Your non-dominant hand is palm up, and your dominant hand is palm down. Slide your dominant hand down the palm of your non-dominant hand, sliding off the fingertips.

My table and chair were cheap.

MY

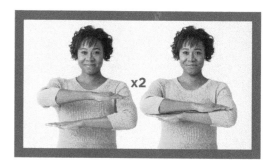

TABLE

CHAIR

IT

CHEAP

MY: Your dominant hand is in the flat B handshape, and you place it on your chest, just under the collarbone.

TABLE: Both hands are in the flat B handshape. Bring your arms up in front of your body, parallel to the ground. Your dominant arm is over the non-dominant hand. Bring the arms together for two short taps.

CHAIR: Both hands are in the H handshape, palms down. Tap your dominant fingers on top of the non-dominant fingers two times.

IT: With your dominant hand in the 1 handshape, point to the side. You can point in a specific direction if it applies. If it's a general use of the sign, point off to the side of your dominant hand.

CHEAP: Both hands are in the flat B handshape. Your non-dominant hand is palm to the side, held horizontally. The dominant hand is palm down. Bring your hand down swiping the palm of your non-dominant hand with the edge of your dominant hand.

> **Memory Tip:** CHEAP is signed in an arch similar to the shape of C, and the motion feels like you're slashing prices at a big bargain store.

My door broke. Can you please help me fix it?

DOOR

IT

BREAK

you-HELP-me

PLEASE?

DOOR: Both hands are in the B handshape, palms out and thumbs together in front of your body. Hinge your dominant hand backward twice like you're opening and closing a door a few times.

IT: With your dominant hand in the 1 handshape, point to the side. You can point in a specific direction if it applies. If it's a general use of the sign, point off to the side of your dominant hand.

BREAK: Both hands are in the S handshape, palms down, and your hands together in front of your body. Twist your wrists in opposite directions as if you were snapping a stick in half.

you-HELP-me: HELP is a directional verb. You can sign it on its own, or you can sign it with a specific direction to add to the meaning. First, let's learn the sign; then I'll show you show to make it directional. HELP is signed with the non-dominant hand in the flat B handshape and the dominant hand in the open A handshape. Place the bottom of your open A hand with the thumb up toward the ceiling in the middle of your flat B hand. Raise your non-dominant hand upward in two short motions.

To make it directional, you can first sign HELP without the upward movements by holding the sign near your body and then arch it toward the person you are wanting to help. If you want the person to help you, start the sign out from your body and arch it toward yourself.

PLEASE: Your dominant hand is in the open B handshape. Place it on your chest underneath your collarbone, and circle your hand starting in a downward motion.

Memory Tip: PLEASE looks like putting your hand to your heart to plead with someone.

Related Vocabulary

HOME: Your dominant hand is in the flat O handshape. Place the fingertips of your hand at the side of your mouth and then arch back, stopping in front of your ear.

Memory Tip: This sign indicates where you eat and where you sleep.

WELCOME: Your dominant hand is in the open B handshape, palm up. Hold the hand out away from your body, off to your dominant side. Bring the hand in toward your torso. Other meanings: INVITE or HIRE.

Memory Tip: This sign looks like opening your door and showing someone into your home with a flourish.

HOUSE: Both hands are in the open B handshape, palms facing each other and fingertips touching. Move both hands apart and down in one motion.

Memory Tip: The sign shows the roof and the walls of the house.

COUCH: This is a combination of CHAIR and showing the shape of a couch. First sign CHAIR, but only tap it once. Show the shape of a couch with both hands in the C handshape, palms down, the sides of your hands touching. Pull both hands away from each other in opposite directions.

Memory Tip: In this sign, you are outlining the shape of a long couch with your C hands.

Activity

Draw a simple blueprint of your living room. Point to each chair, table, couch, door, and so on, and sign the appropriate sign for each item.

Day 18: In the Kitchen

Time: 10–15 minutes

Here you'll learn common signs for the kitchen, including signs for different meals and the all-important compliments to the chef. You'll learn how to ask what's for breakfast, lunch, and dinner and also how to create a menu.

This is a good time to mention that there are not a lot of signs for different food dishes. There are base signs such as eggs, meat, milk, and cheese, but if you want to get specific—inquiring about chicken fettuccini Alfredo, coconut lime shrimp skewers, and the like—you'll need to fingerspell. One trick is to sign the base sign and then fingerspell the rest. For instance, sign CHICKEN and then fingerspell F-E-T-T-U-C-C-I-N-I A-L-F-R-E-D-O.

The food looks good!

FOOD

IT

APPEAR

GOOD

FOOD: This is EAT, signed twice. Bring the flat O handshape up to your lips and tap twice.

IT: With your dominant hand in the 1 handshape, point to the side. You can point in a specific direction if it applies. If it's a general use of the sign, point to the side of your dominant hand.

APPEAR: Your dominant hand is in the 1 handshape. With the tip of your finger, palm facing in, trace a circle around your face. You're not touching your face, but just in front of it. Other meaning: LOOK (as in looks).

GOOD: With both hands in the open B handshape, place the tips of the fingers of the dominant hand on your chin. Bring the hand down to land on the palm of the non-dominant hand.

Memory Tip: This sign is similar to THANK YOU—a reminder that you're thanking someone for doing or offering something good.

What are you cooking for dinner?

DINNER

YOU

x2

COOK

WHAT?

DINNER: Dinner is a combination sign of EAT and NIGHT. You sign EAT with the flat O handshape brought to your lips once. Sign this once, and then quickly sign NIGHT. The non-dominant hand is in the flat B handshape. Your non-dominant arm is held in front of the body horizontally. The dominant hand is in the bent B handshape. Place the wrist of the dominant hand on top of the non-dominant hand, with the fingertips over the edge, pointing toward the floor.

YOU: The dominant hand is in the 1 handshape. Point to the person you are referring to.

COOK: Both hands are in the open B handshape. Your non-dominant hand is palm up, and your dominant hand is palm down. Place your dominant hand on the palm of your non-dominant hand, and then flip the dominant hand palm up and then back to palm down.

Memory Tip: The sign for COOK resembles flipping food in a frying pan.

WHAT: Both hands are in the bent 5 handshape, palms facing up. Shake your hands side to side and furrow your eyebrows while bending your hand forward.

Related Vocabulary

KITCHEN: Sign COOK with both hands in the open B handshape. Your non-dominant hand is palm up, and your dominant hand is palm down. Place your dominant hand on the palm of your non-dominant hand, and then flip the dominant hand palm up and then back to palm down. Then sign ROOM with both hands in the open B hand-shape, hands held horizontal and palms both facing you. Your dominant hand is in front of your non-dominant hand. Bend both wrists back at the same time so that now both palms are facing each other.

Memory Tip: This sign is a combination sign of the COOK and ROOM signs.

BREAKFAST: Sign EAT with your dominant hand in the flat O handshape. Touch your fin-gertips to your mouth once. Sign MORNING with both hands in the flat B handshape. Your non-dominant arm is held horizontally in front of the body. Your dominant hand palm is facing up. Place the fingertips of the non-dominant hand on top of the crook of the elbow of the dominant hand. Raise the dominant arm from horizontal to slightly up, just under a 45-degree angle.

Memory Tip: This is a combination sign of EAT and MORNING.

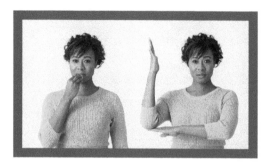

LUNCH: Sign EAT with your dominant hand in the flat O handshape. Touch your fingertips to your mouth one time. Sign NOON with both hands in the flat B handshape. Your non-dominant arm is held horizontally in front of the body. Place the elbow on top of the fingertips of the non-dominant hand. Your dominant arm should be vertical, with the fingertips pointed up.

Memory Tip: This is a combination sign of EAT and NOON.

BAKE: Both hands are in the open B handshape. Your non-dominant hand is palm down in front of your body, just off to the side. Your dominant hand is palm up. Slide your dominant hand forward, underneath your non-dominant hand.

Memory Tip: The motion looks like sliding a tray of cookies into the oven.

Activity

Create a menu for breakfast, lunch, and dinner. Sign the name of the meal (e.g., BREAKFAST), and then fingerspell specifically what you'll be eating for that meal. For an added challenge, invent a menu for the next three days.

Day 19: In the Community

Today, we're going to add more occupational words and phrases to your vocabulary. It's useful to learn lots of different occupational vocabulary, as there are many ways to earn a living that come up in our everyday conversational needs.

She likes her doctor.

HER

DOCTOR

SHE

LIKE

HER: Your dominant hand is in the flat B handshape, palm out at a 45-degree angle. Point the palm to the side. If you're talking about a specific person and they are near you, point the palm toward that person.

DOCTOR: Both hands are in the open B handshape. Your non-dominant hand is horizontal, with your palm facing out at a 45-degree angle. Your dominant hand bends in the bent B handshape and taps the wrist of your non-dominant hand twice.

Memory Tip: The sign for DOCTOR shows someone taking a pulse.

SHE: With your dominant hand in the 1 handshape, point to the side. You can point in a specific direction if it applies. If it's a general use of the sign, point to the side of your dominant hand.

LIKE: Your dominant hand is in the open 8 handshape with your thumb and middle finger resting against your chest. Pull your hand out and away from the body, and as you do, bring the thumb and middle finger together into the 8 handshape.

My son's teacher's name is _____.

MY

SON

HIS

TEACHER

NAME

fs PERSON'S
NAME

MY: With your dominant hand in the flat B handshape, place it on your chest, just under the collarbone.

SON: Both hands are in the flat B handshape. Your non-dominant hand is palm up in front of your body, as if holding a baby. Start with the dominant hand touching the side of the forehead with the side of your index finger, with the palm down. Bring the dominant hand down on top of the non-dominant arm, landing palm up.

HIS: Your dominant hand is in the flat B handshape, palm out at a 45-degree angle. Point the palm to the side. If you're talking about a specific person and they are near you, point the palm toward that person.

TEACHER: This sign is a combination of TEACH and PERSON. Both of your hands are in the flat O handshape, palms facing in and held in front of your head. Push the hands out in a short movement. Sign PERSON by holding both hands in the open B handshape, hands out in front of you, palms facing each other. Draw the hands straight down.

Memory Tip: TEACH represents the person taking knowledge out of their minds and giving it to someone else.

NAME: Both hands are in the H handshape. Hold both hands horizontally, forming an X shape with your dominant hand on top of the non-dominant hand's fingers. Tap the dominant hand twice.

Related Vocabulary

MANAGER: This is a combination of MANAGE and PERSON. Sign MANAGE by holding both hands in the X handshape, palms facing the sides and hands horizontal. Move both hands forward and backward in short alternating movements. Sign PERSON by holding both hands in the open B handshape, hands out in front of you, palms facing each other. Draw the hands straight down. The pulling motion resembles holding the reins on a horse and pulling them to direct it..

LAWYER: This is a combination of LAW and PERSON. The sign for LAW is done with the non-dominant hand in the open B handshape, palm to the side. The dominant hand is in the L handshape. Place the L hand on the top portion of the palm, and then tap the bottom portion of the palm. Sign PERSON by holding both hands in the open B handshape, hands out in front of you, palms facing each other. Draw the hands straight down. The flat hand in the sign LAW represents paper, and the L shows the important words written on it.

FIREFIGHTER: Your dominant hand is in the B handshape, palm out. Tap the back of your hand to your forehead.

Memory Tip: This tapping motion indicates the front of a firefighter's helmet.

POLICE OFFICER: Place your dominant hand in the C handshape over your heart, palm facing the side. If you are left-handed, place the hand over the right side of your chest.

Memory Tip: This motion indicates the badge on a police officer's chest.

Activity

Combine your family members with an occupation. You can use your real family members or invent a family member and occupation. Sign each in this order:

1. Title (mom, dad, son)

2. Fingerspell their name

3. Their occupation

Day 20: At Work

Today, you'll learn a variety of signs to use when signing about work and while you're at work. While "work" can mean lots of things to different people, here are some common terms you might expect to find in an office environment.

I go to work every day.

DAILY

WORK

I

GO

DAILY: Your dominant hand is in the open A handshape, palm facing the side. Place the palm side along your cheek and slide it down toward your mouth twice. Other meaning: EVERY DAY.

WORK: Both hands are in the S handshape, palms down. Tap the heel of your dominant hand on the edge of the non-dominant hand twice. WORK is signed as if you were hammering an iron repeatedly.

I: Your dominant hand is in the 1 handshape. Touch the middle of your chest with your fingertip.

GO: Both hands are in the 1 handshape. Start with both hands held vertically, the hands angled to the side of your dominant hand. In a sharp movement, bring them both down at the same time, ending with your palms facing the ground.

My department has a meeting this afternoon.

NOW

AFTERNOON

MY

DEPARTMENT

MEETING

HAVE

NOW: Both hands are in the Y handshape, palms facing up. Bring the hands down quickly one time.

Memory Tip: Remember, your body is a timeline in ASL. The past is behind, the future is out in front, and the present is right next to your body. NOW is signed right in front of your stomach, which is as close to the present marker on the time-line as you can get.

AFTERNOON: Both hands are in the flat B handshape. Your non-dominant arm is held in front of the body horizontally. The forearm of the dominant hand rests on the fingertips of the non-dominant arm, with the dominant arm at a 45-degree angle.

MY: Your dominant hand is in the flat B handshape, and you place it on your chest, just under the collarbone.

DEPARTMENT: Both hands are in the D handshape, starting in front of your body with the D hands together, palm out. Trace a circle with your hands ending with the D's together on the pinky side with the palms in.

MEETING: Your hands are in a modified 5 handshape. Bring your hands together in front of you with the thumbs touching and the remaining fingers pointed up. Bring the fingertips together to meet above your thumbs. Tap them together twice. Please note: This is for a gathering of people, not to meet someone.

Memory Tip: MEETING shows two groups of people sitting around a long table, their heads coming together to work together.

HAVE: Both hands are in the bent B hand-shape. Bring the fingertips to your chest, right where suspenders would go. This is a firm movement.

YOUR

BOSS

NAME

WHAT?

YOUR: Your dominant hand is the flat B handshape. Hold this handout at a slight angle with the palm pointing toward the person you're referencing.

BOSS: Your dominant hand is in the bent 5 handshape. Tap your dominant shoulder twice with your hand on top of the shoulder.

Memory Tip: BOSS shows the epaulet that a commander wears on their uniform.

NAME: Both hands are in the H handshape. Hold both hands horizontally forming an X shape with your dominant hand on top of the non-dominant hand's fingers. Tap the dominant hand twice.

WHAT: Both hands are in the bent 5 handshape, palms facing up. Shake your hands side to side and furrow your eyebrows while bending your hand forward.

I'll give you a file.

FILE

I

GIVE-you

FILE: Both hands are in the open B hand-shape. The non-dominant hand is vertical with the palm facing the side. The dominant hand is horizontal, palm facing in. Slide the dominant hand between the middle and ring fingers of the non-dominant hand. This sign can be used for digital or physical files.

Memory Tip: FILE shows sliding papers into a file folder.

I: Your dominant hand is in the 1 handshape. Touch the middle of your chest with your fingertip.

GIVE-you: Your dominant hand is in the X handshape, and you move the hand from in front of yourself toward the person you are signing to.

Related Vocabulary

OFFICE: Both hands are in the O hand-shape, hands horizontal and palms facing in. Hold your dominant hand in front of your non-dominant hand. Bend your wrists so that your palms are now facing one another.

Memory Tip: O is for office, and both of your hands are showing the four walls that make up a room.

EMAIL: Your non-dominant hand is in the flat C handshape, palm to the side. Your dominant hand is in the 1 handshape. Start with the dominant hand's finger pointing toward your body, and then swipe it forward in the open space of the C hand so that the finger ends pointing at a forward angle.

Memory Tip: You are showing that the sent digital file is now contained in an inbox of your non-dominant hand.

SEND (electronically): Your dominant hand starts in the baby O handshape with the palm down. Flick your index finger out, and slightly move your hand forward as you do.

Memory Tip: This shows you clicking a button and the document being sent through the air to its recipient.

Activity

Add further detail to the following signs by fingerspelling its associate descriptor. Do this one to three times until you are comfortable signing this specific office element.

OFFICE + fingerspell the name of the office

EMAIL + fingerspell the subject line or the sender and recipient

FILE + file name

BOSS + title and name

DEPARTMENT + department name

Day 21: Around Town

In today's lesson, you'll learn a variety of places that you might frequent in a city or town.

Where do your children go to school?

YOUR

CHILDREN

SCHOOL

GO

WHERE?

YOUR: Your dominant hand is in the flat B handshape. Hold the hand out at a slight angle with the palm pointing toward the person you're referencing.

CHILDREN: Both hands are in the flat B handshape, palms down, held in front of the body with the hands close together. Bounce your hands apart two times.

Memory Tip: The sign for CHILDREN looks like patting the heads of several small children standing in front of you.

SCHOOL: Both hands are in the open B handshape, with the non-dominant hand palm up and the dominant hand palm down. Clap your dominant hand over the palm of your non-dominant hand twice.

GO: Both hands are in the 1 handshape. Start with both hands held vertically and angled to the side of your dominant hand. In a sharp movement, bring them both down at the same time, ending with your palms facing the ground.

WHERE: Hold your dominant hand up in the 1 handshape, palm out. Shake your finger side to side while furrowing your eyebrows and tilting your head.

My husband is going to the city.

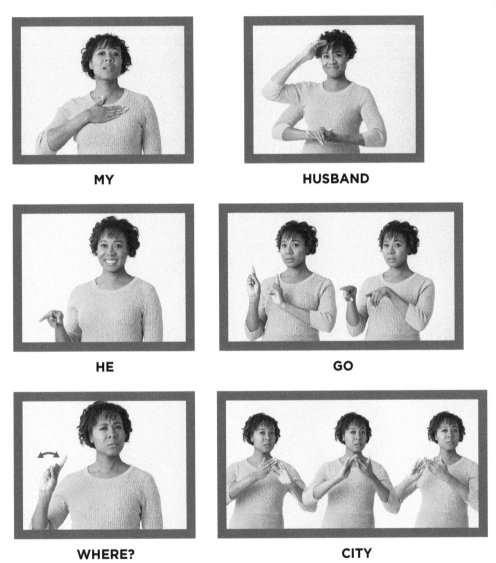

MY

HUSBAND

HE

GO

WHERE?

CITY

MY: With your dominant hand in the flat B handshape, place it on your chest just under the collarbone.

HUSBAND: both hands are in the open C handshape. The non-dominant hand is palm up in front of the body and the dominant hand is palm out, starting at the side of the forehead. Bring the dominant hand down into the clasp of the non-dominant hand.

HE: With your dominant hand in the 1 hand-shape, point to the side. You can point in a specific direction if it applies. If it's a general use of the sign, point off to the side of your dominant hand.

GO: Both hands are in the 1 handshape. Start with both hands held vertically, the hands angled to the side of your dominant hand. In a sharp movement, bring them both down at the same time, ending with your palms facing the ground.

WHERE: Hold your dominant hand up in the 1 handshape, palm out. Shake your finger side to side while furrowing your eyebrows and tilting your head.

CITY: Both hands are in the open B hand-shape, palms facing each other, fingertips together. Twist your hands in.

> **Memory Tip:** CITY shows the roofs of many buildings squished together in one spot.

Related Vocabulary

STORE: Both hands are in the flat O handshape, palms down and in front of your body. Flick your wrists up twice.

SYNAGOGUE: Your non-dominant hand is in the S handshape, palm down. Your dominant hand is in the T handshape, palm out. Tap the base of your T hand on the back of your S hand twice.

CHURCH: Your non-dominant hand is in the S handshape, palm down. Your dominant hand is in the C handshape, palm out. Tap the thumb of your C hand on the back of your S hand twice.

LIBRARY: Your dominant hand is in the L handshape, palm out and held in front of the body. Circle the hand two times.

Activity

Draw a simple map of your neighborhood, identifying various buildings found in today's vocabulary. Sign each building as you come to it. After you sign each place, fingerspell its name. (For instance, STORE S-A-N-D-Y-S.)

Day 22: From A to B

In today's lesson, you'll learn signs to help you reach your destination and ask for directions.

What time are you leaving?

YOU

LEAVE

TIME?

YOU: The dominant hand is in the 1 hand-shape. Point toward the person you are referring to.

LEAVE: Your dominant hand begins in the 5 handshape, palm to the side, and held up above your shoulder. Pull your hand out, away from your body, toward the side, closing into the flat O handshape.

TIME (what time): You sign TIME with your non-dominant hand in the S handshape. Your dominant hand is in the 1 handshape, with a slight bend. Tap your finger on your wrist once, where your watch would be. When you're asking the question "What time?," tap your wrist and twist with a slight pause after your second tap. To make it a question, furrow your eyebrows and tilt your head forward.

> **Memory Tip:** You are tapping your wrist where your watch is placed.

ARRIVE

HOW?

fs
DESTINATION

ARRIVE: Both hands are in the open B handshape. Hold your non-dominant hand out, palm up. Your dominant hand starts palm in and arcs forward and down, slowly, landing on non-dominant palm.

> **Memory Tip:** ARRIVE shows you in one place, jumping to the final location.

HOW: Both hands are in the bent B handshape, knuckles together and palms facing in. Twist your dominant wrist to end with your palm up. Furrow your eyebrows and lean your head forward slightly.

That intersection has traffic.

THAT

INTERSECTION

TRAFFIC

IT

HAVE

THAT: There is a generic and specific way to sign THAT. For the general, your dominant hand is in the Y handshape, and your non-dominant hand is in the flat B handshape, palm up. Place the Y hand into the palm of your non-dominant hand. To sign it specifically, only use your dominant hand, and aim your palm in the direction of the subject you're referring to. Your palm starts out and ends palm down.

INTERSECTION: Both hands are in the 1 handshape, hands held horizontally. Your non-dominant hand palm is facing in, and your dominant hand palm is facing the side. Tap the middle of your dominant hand's finger on top of the middle of your non-dominant hand's finger two times. Your fingers will be in the shape of a lowercase T.

TRAFFIC: Both hands are in the 5 handshape, palms down, with the dominant hand in front of the non-dominant hand. Bring your hands forward in two quick stop-and-go movements.

> **Memory Tip:** TRAFFIC shows the masses of cars lined up in multiple lanes moving forward in a stop-and-go fashion.

IT: With your dominant hand in the 1 handshape, point off to the side. You can point in a specific direction if it applies. If it's a general use of the sign, point off to the side of your dominant hand.

HAVE: Both hands are in the bent B handshape. Bring the fingertips to your chest, right where suspenders would go. This is a firm movement.

Related Vocabulary

LEFT: Hold your dominant hand up in the L handshape, then move it toward your left.

Memory Tip: L stands for left.

RIGHT: Hold your dominant hand up in the R handshape, then move it toward your right.

Memory Tip: R stands for right.

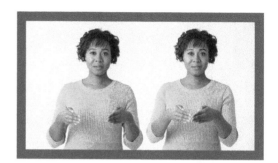

CORNER: Both hands are in the flat B handshape and horizontal. Bring the fingertips of both hands together to form a right angle, or corner, with your hands.

Memory Tip: You're showing two lines meeting together in a point, a corner.

Activity

Look at a map of any location. Start in one location and pick a random location to end further away on the map. Using the streets and various landmarks on the map, walk your imaginary self to your ending destination. As you make your way, sign the directions at each required point. Do you go left or right at the intersection? Turn left at the corner? If you need to go straight, you can sign STRAIGHT with your dominant hand in the B handshape, held vertically in front of your forehead and nose with your palm facing the side. Arch your hand down and forward so that it is now horizontal.

Part II

GRAMMAR

Day 23: Describe-Then-Do

Time: 10 minutes

An expansion technique is something you use to give context to your signs. One easy expansion technique is known as "describe-then-do." To do this, you sign the action that is happening and then, using classifiers, further demonstrate the action. Classifiers are the handshapes used to create signs, but the classifiers themselves are *not* signs. They represent people, places, and objects—and what's happening to or with them.

An easy example is MOM I CALL. In this case, you sign MOM I CALL, using the vocabulary you already know.

Then pick up an imaginary phone using your Y handshape and hold it up to your ear and mime talking into it.

I'm calling my mom.

MOM

I

CALL

This technique is viable for a variety of scenarios. Let's say you want to communicate that you are texting a friend.

You could sign FRIEND I T-E-X-T, using the vocabulary you already know.

I'm texting a friend.

FRIEND

I

T-E-X-T

Then demonstrate you picking up your phone and texting them wildly, thumbs flying across the screen.

This technique works anytime you wish. It adds an added element to your signing that is clear, expressive, and layered. As you have learned throughout your lessons, one of the most important values in ASL communication is clarity.

Activity

Sign these phrases and add your own actions afterward. Don't worry about it being perfect. Trust your gut and go with what feels right. Play around with it, and be sure to check yourself in the mirror.

FILE I GIVE-you

SIGN SLOW PLEASE

MY TABLE IT BREAK

DAILY WORK I GO

Day 24: Adding Emphasis

Time: 20 minutes

Today, you'll learn two additional grammar techniques that add emphasis to your message: reiteration and couching.

REITERATION is when you repeat a sign or phrase for emphasis. What you're signing is important, significant, or has an especially noteworthy impact on you. Here's a sentence without reiteration:

That movie was terrible.

THAT

MOVIE

IT

TERRIBLE

THAT: There is a generic and specific way to sign THAT. For the general, your dominant hand is in the Y handshape, and your non-dominant hand is in the flat B handshape, palm up. Place the Y hand into the palm of your non-dominant hand. To sign it specifically, use only your dominant hand, and aim your palm in the direction of the subject you're referring to. Your palm starts out and ends palm down.

MOVIE: The non-dominant hand is in the flat B handshape, palm facing in, and the dominant hand is in the 5 handshape, palm out. Place the dominant hand behind the non-dominant hand, and shake the dominant hand back and forth.

IT: With your dominant hand in the 1 hand-shape, point off to the side. You can point in a specific direction if it applies. If it's a general use of the sign, point off to the side of your dominant hand.

TERRIBLE: Both hands are in the 8 hand-shape, with the palms facing in and hands held up above the shoulders. Flick your thumb and middle fingers up toward the sky, and your hands ending with all fingers extended up.

Here's the same sentence with reiteration:

That movie was *terrible*!

TERRIBLE

THAT

MOVIE

TERRIBLE

In the reiteration example, the movie was so painful to watch that you had to make sure it was properly communicated. Of course, you would include clear facial expressions to match this experience.

Let's take another look, using vocabulary we already know.

Yesterday, I was sad and cried a lot.

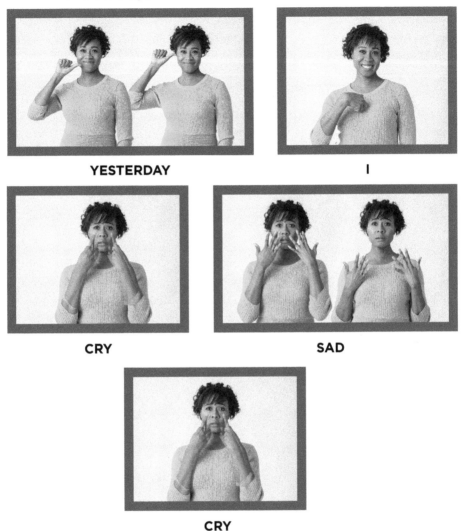

YESTERDAY

I

CRY

SAD

CRY

This sentence uses reiteration very close together. When you use reiteration in this way—repeating a sign as a bookend around a word or group of signs—it draws attention and adds emotional impact to the sign CRY. Signing CRY several times in a row is a technique for pluralizing a word, similar to reiteration, that would show that you were crying a lot. The act of bookending shows the significance or importance of this event. We're not just saying, "I cried a lot," we're showing that it was a very big deal that I did that.

So, what about the second technique? COUCHING makes use of the signing space around you and using classifiers, or you can use ASL handshapes to demonstrate a concept (like you would in charades). You can also use couching by explaining the concept with examples or lists, by contrast, or with a simple explanation. Couching is helpful to know when you're still developing ASL vocabulary because you can use the signs and fingerspelling knowledge you *do* have to communicate something specific or an overarching concept.

Let's try an example. Say you want to tell your friend about a road trip you took up the West Coast. You could do that by couching to give additional meaning to the West Coast.

WEST fsCOAST: WASHINGTON, OREGON, CALIFORNIA

In this example, it's likely that your friend knows what the West Coast is, but you're giving additional meaning and further clarity to your story with couching. You could then go on to break down the story of your trip one state at a time by referencing each state in your list.

Let's practice another one. Here, the signer is explaining the concept of a tornado, perhaps to explain to a class of children what a tornado is like.

There's a lot of rain (the +s show that you're signing RAIN multiple times) and wind (you'd use your hands and facial expressions to demonstrate the type of wind), it's dark, and it can be scary. Of course, there's a lot more here you could do to explain the concept of the wreckage caused by a tornado. You could indicate that houses and buildings are ruined and there's flooding and show the twisting with your index fingers to show the funnel shape and movement across the land that a tornado makes.

A tornado, you know, has tons and tons of rain, and it's windy, dark, and scary.

TORNADO KNOW? RAIN++ WIND DARK SCARE

While most people know what a tornado is, couching becomes a great technique if you're introducing a concept or subject your audience doesn't know much about. However, you can still use this technique if the other person knows the subject matter, as it provides clarity, a deeper visual understanding of the concept, and added information.

Activity

Part 1: Use the reiteration technique on the following sentences. Remember, you can put the repeated sign at the beginning and end of the sentence or on either side of another sign. Whatever you choose to reiterate, it needs to make a sign sandwich, having at least one sign that is not a referent between the emphasized word.

TRAVEL I DON'T-LIKE

I NERVOUS FEEL

TODAY I SICK I THROW-UP

Part 2: Practice the couching technique with each of the following vocabulary words. For instance, to couch the sign WORK, you could list various types of work or items found at work or explain what you do at work. The same ideas can be applied to PARTY, FAMILY, and KITCHEN. It's okay if you get stuck—do your best, and use fingerspelling when you aren't sure about the vocabulary word. A big part of learning any new language is getting comfortable trying, making mistakes, and doing the best you can with what you've got. It's the only way to get better!

WORK

KITCHEN

PARTY

FAMILY

Day 25: Taking Action

Time: 15 minutes

Action signs are an important building block to ASL sentences. "Action sign" is the ASL way of saying "verb." Any word that is a verb is considered an action sign. The signs you'll learn today are common signs you can use in a variety of conversations.

This lesson is fun because you can begin to play with morphology, which means changing the way you sign something to specify its meaning. For instance, you can sign READ normally or as if you were speed reading or *really* bored with the text. The same goes for many different actions: You can walk slowly or quickly, weave in and out, or stumble. You can shop until you drop or mosey along reluctantly.

The beauty of ASL is that you can alter the meaning of a sign by changing or adding different non-manual markers, such as your pace, body language, and facial expressions. (For example, for READ, you can be bored or excited, speed reading, or falling asleep while reading. But ultimately, you're still reading.) Practice in front of a mirror, looking at each action sign and thinking of different ways you can express it. Don't overthink it—just experiment and see what you come up with!

I went shopping last weekend.

PAST

WEEKEND

I

SHOP

PAST: Your dominant hand is in the open B handshape, palm facing in. Starting in front of your dominant shoulder, move the hand backward toward the space behind you.

WEEKEND: Your non-dominant hand is in the flat B handshape, palm up and in front of your body. The dominant hand is in the 1 handshape, palm down, placed at the heel of the palm of your non-dominant hand. Slide your dominant hand down the palm toward the fingertips. When you reach the fingertips, bring your dominant hand down toward the floor.

Memory Tip: WEEKEND looks like tracing the week on a calendar, with the hands dropping off on the last two days of the week.

I: Point to yourself, touching your chest, with your dominant hand in the 1 handshape.

SHOP: The non-dominant hand is in the open B handshape, palm up and in front of the body. The dominant hand is in the flat O handshape, palm up and on top of the palm of your non-dominant hand. Slide your dominant hand down and off the non-dominant hand twice with a small and quick movement.

We both enjoy walking.

US-TWO

ENJOY

WHAT?

WALK

US-TWO: The dominant hand is in the 2 handshape, palm facing up and held in front of the body. Move your hand back and forth toward the person you're addressing, with your index finger and your middle finger pointing toward yourself.

ENJOY: Both of your hands are in the open B handshape. Place your dominant hand on your chest and your non-dominant hand on your stomach. Circle your hands, with your dominant hand circling clockwise and your non-dominant hand circling counterclockwise.

WHAT: Both hands are in the relaxed 5 handshape, palms up. Shake your hands side to side while furrowing your eyebrows and leaning your head forward.

WALK: Both of your hands are in the open B handshape, with palms down in front of your body. Alternate moving your hands forward, as if you are taking steps.

Memory Tip: WALK shows feet taking steps forward.

Related Vocabulary

FLY: Your dominant hand is in the I-L, or PLANE, handshape. Your palm is angled down, and your hand is up near your shoulder. Arch your hand forward to simulate a flying motion.

Memory Tip: You're showing a plane flying across the sky.

SEE: Your dominant hand is in the 2 handshape, palm in. Place the tip of the middle finger underneath the eye and move your hand forward.

Memory Tip: You're showing your eyes looking at something.

READ: Your non-dominant hand is in the open B handshape, palm up at a 45-degree angle. Your dominant hand is in the 2 handshape, palm down. Hold your dominant hand in front of the non-dominant hand and bend your wrist up and down.

Memory Tip: The bottom hand is the book. Your dominant hand and your eyes are going up and down the page, like you're reading.

CHAT: Both hands are in the bent 5 handshape, palms angled up. Shake both hands down at an angle twice.

Memory Tip: You're showing a signer chatting casually with their hands flying during a conversation.

Activity

Sign each action sign, and then fingerspell an associated noun. If you sign READ, fingerspell the title of an article or a book. If you sign CHAT, fingerspell the name of the person you're chatting with. If you sign WALK, where are you walking to? Fingerspell the name of the store where you're going to shop or what you'll purchase when you're there.

Day 26: Tenses

In English, we shift tenses by changing individual words—for instance, "I eat" versus "I ate." In ASL, we add tense to the beginning of a sentence, and it applies to the entire sentence. What's more, your body and its surrounding space are a timeline in sign language. Behind your body is the past, immediately in front of your body is the present, and farther out in front of you is the future. This makes the process of signing tenses fairly intuitive!

    Today, you'll learn the most common ways to add tense to a sign.

I will go on vacation.

WILL　　　　　　　**VACATION**

I　　　　　　　**GO**

WILL: Your dominant hand is in the open B handshape, palm facing to the side. Hold your hand up above your shoulder by your head. Arch the hand up and forward with your hand ending horizontal. Other meanings: FUTURE or WILL (as a question).

VACATION: Both hands are in the 5 handshape. Tap the thumbs onto your chest, a few inches from your armpits, two times. Other meanings: HOLIDAY or RETIRE.

Memory Tip: Visualize a person wearing overalls and sticking their thumbs under the suspenders.

I: Point to yourself, touching your chest, with your dominant hand in the 1 handshape.

GO: Both hands are in the 1 handshape. Start with both hands held vertically, the hands angled to the side of your dominant hand. In a sharp movement, bring them both down at the same time, ending with your palms facing the ground.

It was fall.

RECENT

IT

FALL

RECENT: Your dominant hand is in the X handshape, with your palm facing in. Place the side of your X on your chin near your mouth. Your mouth is open in a clenched teeth expression.

IT: With your dominant hand in the 1 handshape, point off to the side. You can point in a specific direction if it applies. If it's a general use of the sign, point off to the side of your dominant hand. Other meanings: HE or SHE.

FALL: Your non-dominant arm is bent, with the hand held up by your shoulder. Your dominant hand is in the flat B handshape with the side of the index finger resting on the elbow. Brush your elbow twice in a downward motion.

Memory Tip: The brushing motion of the dominant hand is like the leaves falling off the "branch" of your non-dominant arm.

It is spring.

NOW

IT

SPRING

NOW: Both hands are in the Y handshape, palms facing up. Bring the hands down quickly one time. Other meanings: THIS (e.g., "this week") or IMMEDIATELY.

> **Memory Tip:** NOW is signed right in front of your stomach, which is close to the present marker on the timeline.

IT: With your dominant hand in the 1 handshape, point to the side. You can point in a specific direction if you need to indicate one. Point to the side of your dominant hand in general uses of the sign.

SPRING: Your non-dominant hand is in the flat C handshape, palm facing the side. Your dominant hand is in the flat O handshape, palm up. Place the fingertips of the flat O hand in the space between the flat C hand. Push your hand up through the opening, and as you do, open the hand into a 5 hand in a cone shape. Repeat this motion one more time. Other meanings: GARDEN or PLANT.

> **Memory Tip:** The sign for SPRING shows a plant growing out of the ground.

Related Vocabulary

SOON: Your dominant hand is in the F handshape, palm facing in and hand held horizontally. Place the circled fingers on your chin, just underneath your bottom lip. Your mouth is in a pursed O shape, as if you were blowing out your candles.

FINISH: Both hands are in the 5 handshape, palms in with the hands up in front of the shoulder area. Flip your wrists out toward the sides, ending with your palms out. Other meaning: APPLAUSE.

Memory Tip: Imagine finishing an eating competition and then raising your hands to show you're finished and the food is gone.

PAST: Used for any point on the timeline that is now behind you. Your dominant hand is in the open B handshape, palm facing in. Start in front of your dominant shoulder, and then move the hand backward toward the space behind you.

Memory Tip: Your hand is motioning toward what is behind you—in this case, the past.

Activity

Let's play around with tenses now, without worrying if they make sense. Add any tense from today's lesson to the phrases and signs you've learned so far.

Remember: If you're adding a tense to a phrase, the tense sign is the *first* sign. For example, PAST ASL I LEARN is "I learned ASL." When you use tense with a single sign, place the tense sign just in front of it; for example, FINISH LEARN is "I learned." Do this with each sign and each phrase you've learned so far. Consider coming back to this activity when you've learned more.

Day 27: Time and Tense

Time: 15 minutes

Time is an important element of ASL grammar. In today's lesson, you'll expand your vocabulary around time and its relationship to tense. You'll learn to discuss a variety of chunks of time that come up on a regular basis.

I successfully achieved my goal last weekend!

PAST

WEEKEND

GOAL

I

ACCOMPLISH

SUCCESS!!

PAST: Your dominant hand is in the open B handshape, palm facing in. Starting in front of your dominant shoulder, move the hand backward toward the space behind you.

WEEKEND: Your non-dominant hand is in the flat B handshape, palm up, and in front of your body. The dominant hand is in the 1 handshape, palm down, placed at the heel of the palm of your non-dominant hand. Slide your dominant hand down the palm toward the fingertips. When you reach the fingertips, bring your dominant hand down toward the floor.

GOAL: Both of your hands are in the 1 hand-shape. Hold your non-dominant hand up above your shoulder. Your dominant hand is held lower palm facing the side. Bend your wrist so that your dominant hand finger is now pointing at the tip of your non-dominant hand. They do not touch. It's important that your non-dominant hand is higher up than your dominant hand.

I: Point to yourself, touching your chest, with your dominant hand in the 1 handshape.

Memory Tip: When you sign GOAL, your non-dominant hand is up, at your ending location, and your dominant hand starts lower, at your starting location. You're aiming to move from the lower spot to the higher spot.

ACCOMPLISH: The non-dominant hand is in the 1 handshape held up above your head, on your non-dominant side. Start with your dominant hand in the 5 handshape. It starts in front of your body and reaches up to the top of your 1 hand. As it reaches the top, it closes into the S handshape.

SUCCESS/PAH: Both of your hands are in the 1 handshape. Place the tips of your index fingers, palms in, on the sides of your chin. In a grand motion, twist your wrists open and bring your hands up, ending with your palms out. As you sign this, your mouth is saying PAH without making the sounds. Other meaning: PAH! ("finally," as an announcement).

I drove in the country yesterday.

YESTERDAY

COUNTRY

I

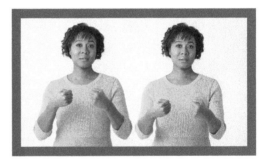

DRIVE

YESTERDAY: The dominant hand is in the open A handshape. The palm is facing forward, and the thumb is at the side of the chin close to the cheek. Tap this spot, and in an arching movement, tap the upper cheek near the ear.

COUNTRY: Hold your non-dominant arm up with your hand near your shoulder. Your dominant hand is in the open B handshape, placed on the elbow. Move your hand in a circle two times on the elbow. Other meaning: COUNTRY (as in a nation).

I: Point to yourself, touching your chest, with your dominant hand in the 1 handshape.

DRIVE: Both hands are in the S handshape, hands horizontal and palms facing in. Push your hands forward in a slight arch.

Memory Tip: DRIVE is showing your hands on the steering wheel, and the motion forward is showing the car moving forward as you drive.

Is the party today or tomorrow?

PARTY

IT

TODAY

TOMORROW

WHICH

PARTY: Both hands are in the Y hand-shape, arms held out horizontally in front of the body. Move both hands side to side in tandem.

IT: With your dominant hand in the 1 hand-shape, point to the side. You can point in a specific direction if it applies. If it's a general use of the sign, point off to the side of your dominant hand.

TODAY: Both hands are in the Y hand-shape, palms up. Hold the hands in front of your body and tap the hands downward two times.

TOMORROW: The dominant hand is in the open A handshape. Start with the thumb on the side of the cheek with the knuckles facing up. Arch the thumb off the cheek toward the space in front of you, ending in a thumbs-up position.

WHICH: Both hands are in the open A hand-shape, palms facing one another. Move the hands up and down in an alternating motion while furrowing the eyebrows.

Memory Tip: The hands move up and down for WHICH, as if asking, "Which hand are you going to choose?"

Related Vocabulary

WEEK: The non-dominant hand is in the flat B handshape, the dominant hand in the 1 handshape, palm up. Place the dominant hand on the palm of the non-dominant hand, and slide the hand down the palm toward the fingertips.

> **Memory Tip:** Your bottom hand is a calendar, and your top hand is sliding across one row, indicating one week.

MONTH: Both hands are in the 1 handshape. Your non-dominant hand is vertical with palm facing out. The dominant hand is horizontal with palm facing you. In a downward movement, drag the dominant hand down the non-dominant hand.

> **Memory Tip:** The MONTH motion shows the finger sliding down the calendar page.

YEAR: Both hands are in the S handshape. Place the dominant hand on top of the non-dominant hand with both hands held horizontally. Circle the dominant hand forward and around the non-dominant hand to land back on top of the non-dominant hand.

Memory Tip: The YEAR motion represents the earth traveling around the sun.

Activity

Pull up your calendar and find each different unit of time: a week, a month, a year, yesterday, today, and tomorrow. Point to each unit on the calendar and sign them. Do this at least two times for each unit of time.

Day 28: Sentence Structure

Time: 20 minutes

ASL grammar is quite different from English grammar. Today's lesson will teach you the basic sentence structure to use in your ASL sentences. In the previous lessons, you learned ASL grammar without realizing it, much like a young child who absorbs new languages, mannerism, and habits. You haven't been introduced to the official grammar rules until now because it's more important for you to get a feel for the way ASL sentences flow. This approach makes it easier for you to learn to sign correct ASL grammar with less mental effort because you'll know what feels right even if you can't define it. You can look to your growing toolkit of vocabulary and phrases to help guide you.

It's likely that if you're able to read this book, English grammar has become second nature to you, but that process took time, as will learning ASL grammar. Practice signing each of the sentences in this book over and over again to help you feel the flow of an ASL sentence. For now, take a closer look at basic sentence structure in the following examples. Doing the activities will help you become more comfortable with sentence structure and make it more natural to create your own.

Let's examine this sentence: "My party is today." In ASL, you would not sign each of these four words. What's more, you would sign them in a completely different word order. In ASL grammar, this sentence is: TODAY MY PARTY.

The basic sentence structure for an ASL sentence is made up of three elements: time, topic, and comment. This is the order of those elements:

TIME + TOPIC + COMMENT

TIME: You learned in a previous lesson that tense goes at the beginning of each sentence. The tense, in this case, is TODAY.

TOPIC: The main subject of each sentence—in this case, PARTY.

COMMENT: A supporting sign or signs related to the topic of the sentence—in this case, MY. Comments can be broken into smaller parts for easier sentence building—for example, adjectives, verbs, and negatives. There are many types of comments, and in most cases, your sentences will be filled with them.

Here, we'll look at how to organize comments. Many comments consist of:

ACTION: a verb

NEGATION: a negative sign, such as NO, NOT, WON'T, etc.

When we include comments, sentences can look like any one of the following. Let's look at these examples, using vocabulary we already know.

I enjoyed my party today.

TIME + TOPIC + COMMENT + ACTION

TODAY

MY

PARTY

ENJOY

My party was terrible today.

TOPIC + COMMENT + NEGATION

TODAY

MY

PARTY

TERRIBLE

I don't know if I'll have my party today.

TIME + TOPIC + COMMENT + ACTION + NEGATION

TODAY

MY

PARTY

HAVE

DON'T-KNOW

When creating an ASL sentence, always put your action sign at the end of the sentence. There are two exceptions to this rule. One (like we saw previously) is when you are negating your final sign—for example, RUN WON'T. The other is when asking a question, which you'll learn about in tomorrow's lesson.

You must brush your teeth every day.

TIME + TOPIC + ACTION

DAILY

BRUSH-TEETH

YOU

MUST

I cried yesterday.

TIME + TOPIC + ACTION

YESTERDAY

I

CRY

Something feels wrong.

TOPIC + ACTION + NEGATION

SOMETHING

FEEL

WRONG

My table is cheap.

MY

x2

TABLE

IT

CHEAP

REFERENTS

As a visual language, ASL uses all of the space available to tell a story and to add depth and clarity to any message you share. To ensure that there is maximum clarity, we use referents. In English, referents are pronouns. You'll identify them the same way, but their proper use must be understood.

You'll see more referents in a signed sentence than you'll see in an English sentence because of the visual use of your signing space. When signing about someone or something, you assign them a space around you. Each time you point back to that space, your audience will know you're talking about that person or object. You can add more people and objects to your sentences by pointing to various locations to your right, to your left, and in front of you.

Here is a short list of referent signs:

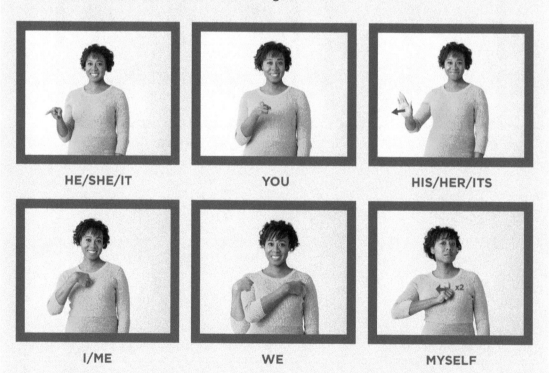

HE/SHE/IT   YOU   HIS/HER/ITS

I/ME   WE   MYSELF

Activity

Write out four simple English statements from Days 3–21—for instance, "I have a brother" or "She went to the store yesterday"—followed by their ASL translations. Go through your ASL translations and label each part of the sentence with the corresponding sentence part. Be sure to also identify your referents.

When you look at creating your own sentences and use the sentence structure templates, there is no exact space to place a referent. Instead, you sign them where they're needed.

Day 29: Unpacking Questions

Time: 15–18 minutes

We learned earlier that when you sign a question, your facial expressions are important. A yes/no question (any question that can be answered with a "yes" or a "no") is signed by raising your eyebrows, tilting your head forward, and holding the question sign for a brief moment. WH-questions (any question that *cannot* be answered with a "yes" or a "no") is signed with furrowed eyebrows and tilted head.

But what about the grammar that's driving these sentences in the first place? In today's lesson, you'll take a closer look at the grammar driving yes/no and WH-questions. This grammar is very specific for ASL questions. Something to note before you get started: No matter the type of question, you always put the QUESTION sign at the end of the sentence. If you have an action or negation in your sentence, you still put the QUESTION sign at the very end.

First, let's look at the basic structure:

TOPIC + COMMENT + QUESTION

If I were to sign STORE YOU GO without raising my eyebrows and pausing slightly at the end as I tilted my head, people would think I was saying, "You are going to the store." If I signed the exact same three signs but raised my eyebrows, tilted my head

forward, and made eye contact with the person I was signing with as I signed GO, I'd now be asking them, "Are you going to the store?"

Are you going to the store?

STORE + YOU + GO

TOPIC + COMMENT + QUESTION

What exactly is a QUESTION? This can be any word that makes the sentence a question. This includes the basic WHO, WHAT, WHERE, WHEN, WHY, and HOW. You can use any action sign (verb) to create a question. BOOK YOU LIKE? YOU SHOP?

Here are a few you can use: VISIT, CELEBRATE, CRY, ARRIVE, FEEL, SHOWER, HAVE. You can use nouns as question signs as well: THAT YOUR HOME? YOU HEALTHY? YOUR CAR PURPLE?

When you are signing a question to someone, think about which word is the question sign. Place that sign at the end of the sentence and use the appropriate facial expressions. You can use the sentences throughout this book to help guide you when identifying these words.

Let's break down a few sentences:

What time are you visiting her family on Saturday?

SATURDAY + HER + FAMILY + YOU + VISIT + TIME?

TIME + REFERENT + TOPIC + REFERENT + ACTION + QUESTION

SATURDAY

HER

FAMILY

YOU

VISIT

TIME?

You didn't go to work yesterday?

YESTERDAY + WORK + YOU + GO + NOT?

TIME + TOPIC + REFERENT + ACTION + NEGATION + QUESTION

YESTERDAY

WORK

YOU

GO

NOT?

Which holiday do you celebrate?

HOLIDAY + YOU + CELEBRATE + WHICH?

TOPIC + REFERENT + ACTION + WH-QUESTION

HOLIDAY

YOU

CELEBRATE

WHICH?

Do your children go to school?

YOUR + CHILDREN + SCHOOL + GO?

REFERENT + TOPIC + COMMENT + Y/N QUESTION

YOUR

CHILDREN

SCHOOL

GO?

When will you visit her family?

HER + FAMILY + YOU + VISIT + WHEN?

REFERENT + TOPIC + REFERENT + ACTION + WH-QUESTION

HER

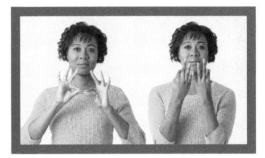

FAMILY

YOU

VISIT

WHEN?

Activity

In the following sentences, replace each WH-question (or HOW) sign with a different WH-question sign. Sign your new question sentences using the correct facial expressions.

VACATION YOU GO WHERE?

DOOR IT BREAK HOW?

DINNER YOU COOK WHAT?

YOUR PARTY WHEN?

HIS FAMILY WHAT-DO?

Look back over the question signs you've identified from earlier lessons and change out the question sign. If it's a WH-question, use a different WH-question sign in the sentence. If it's a yes/no question, change out the sign to anything that will fit. You can even take a statement and turn it into a yes/no question. For instance, DAILY BRUSH-TEETH YOU MUST. You can make that a question by turning MUST into a yes/no question. To sign it, you'll raise your eyebrows, tilt your head, and hold the last sign for a few seconds longer than usual. Hunt around for other sentences you can do this to, and practice signing them as a question.

Day 30: Rhetorical Questions

Time: 15 minutes

In ASL, a rhetorical question involves the speaker asking a WH-question in the middle of their sentence—and then answering it immediately themselves. In the Deaf community, rhetorical questions are common because the sentence structure is quick, intuitive, and relatively easy to master. You'll find them throughout this book because of their frequent use in ASL.

It's important to note that for rhetorical questions, facial expressions are different. As you now know, when you sign a WH-question, you furrow your eyebrows. In a rhetorical question, you raise them. This is an important distinction. With rhetorical questions, the second part of the sentence explains the first part; the question sign bisects the sentence and joins the two parts together. Here is what the rhetorical sentence structure looks like:

TOPIC + QUESTION + COMMENT + ACTION

Now, let's look at an example.

I don't know if it will rain.

RAIN + WILL? + DON'T-KNOW

TOPIC + QUESTION + COMMENT

RAIN

WILL?

DON'T-KNOW

My job is in Nashville.

MY + JOB + WHERE? + N-A-S-H-V-I-L-L-E.

REFERENT + TOPIC + QUESTION + COMMENT

MY

JOB

WHERE?

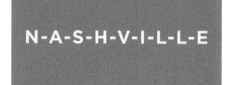

N-A-S-H-V-I-L-L-E

An easy way to think about rhetorical questions is to imagine the question replacing the word "because." Just look at the following example that uses vocabulary you already know.

I need my paycheck **because** I need to buy a plane ticket.

I need a paycheck so that I can buy a plane ticket.

PAYCHECK + I + NEED + WHY + PLANE + TICKET + I + BUY

TOPIC + REFERENT + COMMENT + QUESTION + COMMENT + COMMENT + REFERENT + ACTION

PAYCHECK

I

NEED

FOR FOR

PHRASE CONTINUED >

PLANE

TICKET

I

BUY

To create longer rhetorical sentences, you can also stack two smaller sentences together to make one longer sentence, just as you would a compound sentence in English. The key here is to add a rhetorical question in the middle of the two short sentences. The example you know also uses vocabulary we've covered so far in this book.

I shopped last week because I had a party on Saturday.

LAST-WEEK + I + SHOP + FOR-FOR + SATURDAY + PARTY + I + HAVE

TIME + REFERENT + ACTION + QUESTION + TIME + COMMENT + REFERENT + ACTION

LAST-WEEK

I

SHOP

FOR FOR

SATURDAY

PHRASE CONTINUED >

PARTY **I** **HAVE**

Here, we added the rhetorical question WHY in the place of "because." We also added a smaller sentence at the end to expound on it. Together they make one long sentence.

Activity

Identify the parts of the following sentences. Sign each sentence using the correct facial expression for a rhetorical question.

MY HUSBAND HE GO WHERE? CITY

US-TWO ENJOY WHAT? WALK

YESTERDAY I CRY WHY? SAD UPSET

RAIN WILL? DON'T-KNOW TRUE APPEAR CLOUD WIND

PAYCHECK I NEED WHY? PLANE TICKET I BUY

CONCLUSION

You've made it through all 30 days of lessons. Congratulations! Hopefully, this is only the beginning of your ASL adventure. As you head off into the world and practice (and get comfortable making mistakes), your comfort with and fluency in ASL grammar and vocabulary will only grow.

As you expand your ASL knowledge, be sure to look back over the lessons a few more times to reinforce your learning and to ensure that the vocabulary sticks. If there were any activities you skipped over or would like to repeat—there is no wrong time to revisit them! This book is only the beginning.

As you expand your ASL knowledge, I encourage you to increase your involvement with and support for Deaf community rights—stay curious, don't give up, and be sure to ask a heap of questions to those who live with deafness or hearing impairment.

The list of resources in the back of the book will support your knowledge and involvement. Best of luck—and thank you for going on this journey with me.

RESOURCES

To learn more about ASL and Deaf culture, check out any of the following associations or titles:

National Association of the Deaf: NAD.org

Gallaudet University: Gallaudet.edu/asl-connect

Carroll, Cathryn, and Susan M. Mather. *Movers & Shakers: Deaf People Who Changed the World*

Holcomb, Roy K., Samuel K. Holcomb, and Thomas K. Holcomb. *Deaf Culture, Our Way: Anecdotes from the Deaf Community*

Padden, Carol A., and Tom L. Humphries. *Deaf in America: Voices from a Culture*

Audism Unveiled. **Directed by Ben Bahan, H-Dirksen Bauman, and Facundo Montenegro**

To get involved in your local Deaf community:

Google Search for Deaf coffee chat, Deaf club, and ASL club in your city

Deaf Expos

Deaf Linx: DeafLinx.com

ASLSlam.com

Your local Registry of Interpreters for the Deaf (RID) chapter

Your local colleges or universities may have an ASL Club and will know of the Deaf Community around you.

To learn more ASL:

The American Sign Language Handshape Dictionary **by Richard Tennant**

American Sign Language for Kids: 101 Easy Signs for Nonverbal Communication **by Rochelle Barlow**

The American Sign Language Workbook **by Rochelle Barlow**

The Gallaudet Children's Dictionary of American Sign Language **by Editors of Gallaudet University (Even if you're not a child, this one is extremely useful.)**

The Gallaudet Dictionary of American Sign Language **by Clayton Valli**

ASL Rochelle: ASLRochelle.com

Dawn Sign Press: DawnSign.com

Life Print University: LifePrint.com

INDEX

ACKNOWLEDGMENTS

Thank you to my Mama, my Daddio, my stepparents, my grandparents, my brothers, my sisters, my aunts, my uncles, my cousins, my nieces, and my nephews. Your outpouring of cheering, encouragement, love, and excitement has always been life-changing. I don't know who I bribed to let me be in your family, but I'm so grateful I did.

Thank you to the amazing team of people who made this beautiful book possible: Erin Nelson for being a rock star editor, Meg Baggot for her incredible attention to detail, Emma Hall for making this book both useful and beautiful, James Bueti for his beautiful photography and zest for life, and Jocelynn Only for her beautiful smile and soul. It's been humbling and inspiring to work with y'all.

I'm grateful for the random challenge that had me posting my first ASL video on YouTube (even though the video quality still makes me cringe). I'm grateful for my friends Lauren Weiss and Lisa Voorhees, who made life and ASL fun again back in high school.

Thank you to my ASL Accelerated students, who put a smile on my face every single day and love sign language as much as I do.

Thank you to Nick and my sweet children. There aren't enough words or space in this book for me to express my gratitude.

When you love as many people as I do, deciding whom to dedicate a book to first is a burden. One I wouldn't trade. Don't worry guys, I'll keep writing, and one day, your name will be in the dedication and not just the acknowledgments.

Thank you, thank you, thank you.

ABOUT THE AUTHOR

 **Rochelle Barlow** first began to learn ASL as a young child. She studied and practiced on her own for many years and then with private tutors, in high school classes, and as a Deaf Education student at Utah State University. She worked at the School for the Deaf and Blind in Ogden, Utah, and interpreted after college for various school systems. Rochelle began teaching ASL to families and individuals more than 15 years ago, expanding her instruction to local community centers, co-ops, and private schools and classrooms. She then launched her own business, teaching ASL online at ASL Rochelle. Rochelle loves to read, write, belt out music from the '20s to the '60s, and watch British murder mysteries. She is the mother of six incredible children and lives in southern Oregon.

CPSIA information can be obtained
at www.ICGtesting.com
Printed in the USA
JSHW051911271021
19908JS00004B/6